QUOTES

FROM THE UNDERGROUND

radical wisdom in small doses

WILLIAM MARTIN

Quotes from the Underground
Copyright © 2012, by William Martin.
Cover photograph by Lawrence von Knorr. Used by permission.

FIRST SUNBURY PRESS EDITION
Printed in the United States of America
September 2012

Trade paperback ISBN: 978-1-62006-112-1
Mobipocket format (Kindle) ISBN: 978-1-62006-113-8
ePub format (Nook) ISBN: 978-1-62006-114-5

Published by:
Sunbury Press
Camp Hill, PA
www.sunburypress.com

Camp Hill, Pennsylvania   USA

For my daughter, Casey

Introduction

Quotes from the Underground: Radical Wisdom in Small Doses is a collection of the best insights of the political left. The quotes are edgy and original. They will be an inspiration for writers, researchers, bloggers, activists, freethinkers, liberals, socialists, and anarchists – lefties of all stripes who care about equality, freedom, compassion, and justice.

The title of the book is a play on Dostoevsky's dark 1864 classic *Notes from the Underground*. The book's quotations are antithetical to the outlook of the central character, the angry and self-loathing Underground Man. He is the quintessential misanthrope; he hates reason, science, liberalism and society. If the book were written today, he would hate immigrants, despise women's rights, and want to abolish all forms of welfare except his Social Security check. He would insist that corporations are people, contend that Elvis was still alive, and believe our first black president was born in Kenya. In other words, the Underground Man would fit nicely into today's Tea Party.

Many people like to say that there is no difference between the left and right in American politics. This pose is easy because it relieves us of the burden of thinking, choosing, and acting. It is also untrue. The Tea Party and Occupy Wall Street movements are a case in point. Beyond the rallies and protest signs, the movements are profoundly different. The Tea Party hopes to return America to a pristine past that never existed. Wealthy fat cats underwrite the festivities, and in return they get advocates for less government oversight of corrupt financial institutions and less tax on millionaires and billionaires. Tea Baggers nominally control the Republican Party. Yet many still dress up in wigs and three-pointed hats. They fancy themselves patriots, but they are seen around the world as corporate dupes.

Occupy Wall Street represents the interests of the many, including the poor, unemployed, homeless, and people struggling with overwhelming debt. Occupy activists begin with the demand that the banks be held accountable for triggering our current financial meltdown and end with a vision of a more just, democratic, and egalitarian society. Occupiers don't wear costumes, they don't have deep pockets of cash or control a political party, but they are on the right side of history. Working to reform our broken financial and political institutions, they often endure beatings, arrests, and strip searches. Occupy activists don't have corporate media to sponsor and promote them, but they are our actual patriots.

Quotes from the Underground will appeal not only to those who feel solidarity with the Occupy movement. It will resonate with anyone who wants to engage the critical topics of our time – gay marriage, corporate power, birth control, abortion, health care, education, social media, racism, woman's rights, civil disobedience, voter suppression, religion, globalization, wealth, poverty, hope and much more. Readers will also appreciate the section on "Stupid Rightwing Quotes." It provides a glimpse into the dangerous and dim-witted worldview of modern conservatism.

Read the quotes. Be inspired. Get involved. It has never been more important to be informed and more necessary to achieve social and economic justice.

William Martin
August 2012

Abortion

Abolition of a woman's right to abortion, when and if she wants it, amounts to compulsory maternity: a form of rape by the State.
- Edward Abbey

Being pro-choice is not being pro-abortion. Being pro-choice is trusting the individual to make the right decision for herself and her family, and not entrusting that decision to anyone wearing the authority of government.
- Hillary Clinton

When you peel back the layers of the anti-choice motivation, it always comes back to two things: What is the nature and purpose of human sexuality? And second, what is the role of women in the world?
- Gloria Feldt

Among the first things the Nazis did upon seizing power in 1933 was to outlaw abortion.
- Steven Conn

If men could get pregnant, abortion would be a sacrament.
- Florynce Kennedy

The preservation of life seems to be rather a slogan than a genuine goal of the anti-abortion forces; what they want is control. Control over behavior: power over women.
- Ursula K. Le Guin

No woman wants an abortion as she wants an ice cream cone or a Porsche. She wants an abortion as an animal caught in a trap wants to gnaw off its own leg.
- Frederica Mathewes-Green

We will not return to the back-alley, wire-hanger abortions.
- Deborah Morse-Kahn

A woman is a person; a zygote or a fetus is not.
- Michael Schwalbe

If the anti-abortion movement took a tenth of the energy
they put into noisy theatrics and devoted it to improving
the lives of children who have been born into lives of
poverty, violence, and neglect, they could make a world
shine.
- Michael Jay Tucker

Against abortion? Don't have one.
- Unknown

Abortion, for many women, is more than an experience of
suffering beyond anything most men will ever know; it is
an act of mercy, and an act of self-defense.
- Alice Walker

Activism

Action is the antidote to despair.
- Joan Baez

We are building a democratic movement that will take this country back from the corporate hooligans who have hijacked it from us.
- David Cobb

We must become the change we wish to see in the world.
- Mahatma Gandi

People often say with pride, "I'm not interested in politics." They might as well say, "I'm not interested in my standard of living, my health, my job, my rights, my freedoms, my future or any future."
- Martha Gellhorn

The biggest sin is sitting on your ass.
- Florynce Kennedy

Don't agonize, organize.
- Florynce Kennedy

If we act as if social change for the better is impossible, we guarantee it will be impossible.
- Robert McChesney

Word to the wise: If you are a peace activist, the government may be watching you and reading your e-mails.
- Matthew Rothschild

Activism is the rent I pay for living on this planet.
- Alice Walker

Small acts, when multiplied by millions of people, can transform the world.
- Howard Zinn

Agnosticism

No agnostic ever burned anyone at the stake or tortured a pagan, heretic, or an unbeliever.
- Daniel J. Boorstin

I do not pretend to know where many ignorant men are sure – that is all that agnosticism means.
- Clarence Darrow

I have always considered "Pascal's Wager" a questionable bet to place. Any God worth "believing in" would surely prefer an honest agnostic to a calculating hypocrite.
- Alan Dershowitz

I am an agnostic pagan. I doubt the existence of many gods.
- Unknown

America

I love America because it is a confused, chaotic mess - and I hope we can keep it this way for at least another thousand years. The permissive society is the free society.
- Edward Abbey

I love America more than any other country in the world and, exactly for this reason, I insist on the right to criticize her perpetually.
- James Baldwin

We Americans are not usually thought to be a submissive people, but of course we are. Why else would we allow our country to be destroyed? Why else would we be rewarding its destroyers? Why else would we all — by proxies we have given to greedy corporations and corrupt politicians — be participating in its destruction?
- Wendell Berry

The gravest danger we face as a nation is not from the far right . . . but from a bankrupt liberal class that has lost the will to fight and the moral courage to stand up for what it espouses.
- Chris Hedges

It is ironic that the United States should have been founded by intellectuals, for throughout most of our political history, the intellectual has been for the most part either an outsider, a servant or a scapegoat.
- Richard Hofstadter

We do not need to dominate the world.
- Molly Ivins

We only want, we only ask, that when we stand up and talk about one nation under God, liberty, justice for everybody, we only want to be able to look at the flag, put our right hand over our hearts, repeat those words, and know that they are true.
- Barbara Jordan

It's not just that Americans are scandalously ignorant. It's that they seem to believe they have a democratic right to their ignorance.
- Michael Kinsley

America today is in danger. It faces the threat of domination by a radical, authoritarian right wing that refers to itself as "conservative," as if it were preserving and promoting American values. In fact, it has been trampling on them.
- George Lakoff

Many Americans hunger for a different kind of society -- one based on principles of caring, ethical and spiritual sensitivity, and communal solidarity.
- Michael Lerner

America used to be a country that thought big about the future. Major public projects, from the Erie Canal to the interstate highway system, used to be a well-understood component of our national greatness. Nowadays, however, the only big projects politicians are willing to undertake — with expense no object — seem to be wars.
- Paul Krugman

New Rule: America must stop bragging it's the greatest country on earth, and start acting like it.
- Bill Maher

The American way of life is not sustainable. It doesn't acknowledge that there is a world beyond America.
- Arundhati Roy

America is a corporate welfare state.
- Jane Stillwater

America . . . just a nation of two hundred million used car salesmen with all the money we need to buy guns and no qualms about killing anybody else in the world who tries to make us uncomfortable.
- Hunter S. Thompson

We live in a beautiful country. But people who have no respect for human life, freedom, or justice have taken it over. It is now up to all of us to take it back.
- Howard Zinn

Anarchism

Anarchism is founded on the observation that since few men are wise enough to rule themselves, even fewer are wise enough to rule others.
- Edward Abbey

Anarchism is stateless socialism.
- Mikhail Bakunin

Anarchism means a condition or society where all men and women are free, and where all enjoy equally the benefits of an ordered and sensible life.
- Alexander Berkman

Anarchism is a tendency in the history of human thought and action which seeks to identify coercive, authoritarian, and hierarchical structures of all kinds and to challenge their legitimacy.
- Noam Chomsky

An anarchist is someone who doesn't need a cop to make him behave.
- Ammon Hennacy

We anarchists do not want to emancipate the people; we want the people to emancipate themselves.
- Errico Malatesta

Animal Rights

The question is not, "Can they reason?" nor, "Can they talk?" but rather, "Can they suffer?"
- Jeremy Bentham

The only creature on earth whose natural habitat is a zoo is the zookeeper.
- Robert Brault

I ask people why they have deer heads on their walls. They always say because it's such a beautiful animal. There you go. I think my mother is attractive, but I have photographs of her.
- Ellen DeGeneres

It is inexcusable for scientists to torture animals; let them make their experiments on journalists and politicians.
- Henrik Ibsen

Ask the experimenters why they experiment on animals, and the answer is: "Because the animals are like us." Ask the experimenters why it is morally okay to experiment on animals, and the answer is: "Because the animals are not like us."
- Charles R. Magel

If slaughterhouses had glass walls, everyone would be vegetarian.
- Paul McCartney

Four legs good, two legs bad.
- George Orwell

Hunting is not a sport. In a sport, both sides should know they're in the game.
- Paul Rodriguez

9

If a group of beings from another planet were to land on Earth - beings who considered themselves as superior to you as you feel yourself to be to other animals - would you concede them the rights over you that you assume over other animals?
- George Bernard Shaw

When nonvegetarians say that 'human problems come first' I cannot help wondering what exactly it is that they are doing for human beings that compels them to continue to support the wasteful, ruthless exploitation of farm animals.
- Peter Singer

Apathy

My generation's apathy. I'm disgusted with it. I'm disgusted with my own apathy too, for being spineless and not always standing up against racism, sexism and all those other -isms the counterculture has been whining about for years.
- Kurt Cobain

The world is a dangerous place to live; not because of the people who are evil, but because of the people who don't do anything about it.
- Albert Einstein

I prefer the folly of enthusiasm to the indifference of wisdom.
- Anatole France

These are the days when men of all social disciplines and all political faiths seek the comfortable and the accepted; when the man of controversy is looked upon as a disturbing influence; when originality is taken to be a mark of instability; and when, in minor modification of the original parable, the bland lead the bland.
- John Kenneth Galbraith

The death of democracy is not likely to be an assassination from ambush. It will be a slow extinction from apathy, indifference, and undernourishment.
- Robert M. Hutchins

Atheism

It is not hardness of heart or evil passions that drive certain individuals to atheism, but rather a scrupulous intellectual honesty.
- Steve Allen

Atheists: The Real Ghostbusters
- Anonymous

When I told the people of Northern Ireland that I was an atheist, a woman in the audience stood up and said, "Yes, but is it the God of the Catholics or the God of the Protestants in whom you don't believe?"
- Quentin Crisp

Be thankful that you have a life, and forsake your vain and presumptuous desire for a second one.
- Richard Dawkins

I think atheism and secularism are . . . names that ultimately we don't need. We don't need a name for disbelief in astrology. I don't think we need anything other than rationality and reason and intellectual honesty.
- Sam Harris

We are all atheists with respect to Zeus and Thor.
- Sam Harris

What can be asserted without proof can be dismissed without proof.
- Christopher Hitchins

It does no injury for my neighbor to say there are twenty gods or no God.
- Thomas Jefferson

He was an embittered atheist, the sort of atheist who does not so much disbelieve in God as personally dislike Him.
- George Orwell

We must question the story logic of having an all-knowing all-powerful God, who creates faulty Humans, and then blames them for his own mistakes.
- Gene Roddenberry

Banks

What is robbing a bank compared to founding one?
- Bertolt Brecht

Genteel liberals have allowed American conservatives to all
but monopolize political fury since the banks went down.
- Nick Cohen

It is time for a participatory New Deal, to bring the banks
and corporations under the regulations and reforms they
have escaped through runaway globalization.
- Tom Hayden

I sincerely believe . . . that banking establishments are
more dangerous than standing armies.
- Thomas Jefferson

The captains of high finance are demanding that we reduce
public debt, which we ran up to bail them out . . . That
takes a lot of nerve. First they crash the system and run
away with a fat pocket of cash. Then they demand that we
clean up our financial act or they won't loan out any
money.
- Les Leopold

What can citizens do when the banks start robbing them—
and the political system fails to protect them from
corporate abuses?
- Jake Lewis

I have the Confederacy before me and the bankers behind
me, and I fear the bankers most.
- Abraham Lincoln

Some men rob you with a six-gun - others rob you with a
fountain pen.
 - Woody Guthrie

Barack Obama

If Hillary gave up one of her balls and gave it to Obama,
he'd have two.
- James Carville

Obama came to power in circumstances as grim as those
that greeted Roosevelt in 1932. But he . . . did not
challenge Wall Street's power.
- Nick Cohen

Obama is head of the dysfunctional family that is America
- a rational man running a most irrational nation, a high-
minded man in a low-minded age.
- Maureen Dowd

The imperial projects and the corporate state have not
altered under Obama. The state kills as ruthlessly and
indiscriminately in Iraq, Afghanistan and Pakistan as it did
under Bush.
- Chris Hedges

His opponents remain filled with a passionate intensity,
while his [leftist] supporters, having received no respect,
lack all conviction.
- Paul Krugman

He has a good heart, a good mind, treats people with
dignity, doesn't court conflict and represents the best in
this country.
- Gloria Steinem

The black mascot of Wall Street oligarchs.
- Cornell West, Princeton University philosopher's new view
of Obama

Birth Control

Attacking me and women who use contraception by calling us prostitutes and worse cannot silence us.
- Sandra Fluke, responding to Rush Limbaugh who called her a slut and a prostitute

A photo of a shirtless Rick Santorum lounging in a pool is circulating on the Internet. Ironically, the photo has proven to be a very effective form of birth control.
- Conan O'Brien

It would be a service to mankind if the pill were available in slot machines and the cigarette were placed on prescription.
- Malcolm Potts

No woman can call herself free who does not own and control her body. No woman can call herself free until she can choose consciously whether she will or will not be a mother.
- Margaret Sanger

Books

Beware the man of one book.
- Isaac Disraeli

When I get a little money I buy books; and if any is left I buy food and clothes.
- Erasmus

A book must be an ice-axe to break the seas frozen inside our soul.
- Franz Kafka

It has never been easier to publish a book and it has never been harder to sell one.
- Lawrence Knorr

If there's a book you really want to read but it hasn't been written yet, then you must write it.
- Toni Morrison

How many a man has dated a new era in his life from the reading of a book.
- Henry David Thoreau

Bullying

Whether it is a Republican debate audience booing a gay soldier or Rush Limbaugh's vicious attack on a female Georgetown law student or Newt Gingrich's salvos at the poor, bullying has become boilerplate.
- Charles M. Blow

I was raised to stand up to the bully in the schoolyard, and you don't lose that.
- Barbara Boxer

Based upon the collective behavior of far-right conservative Republicans, we can only deduce that a considerable number of them are bullies and ought to be treated as such.
- Bob Cesca

Nothing can prepare you for living or working with a sociopathic serial bully. It is the most devastating, draining, misunderstood, and ultimately futile experience imaginable.
- Tim Field

Every time a student hears a sexist joke or a racial slur, every time she hears the words 'faggot' or 'slut' or 'fatso' or 'retard,' she must make a decision. Will I be a perpetrator, a victim, a bystander or a human rights defender?
- Kerry Kennedy

Bullies—political bullies, economic bullies, and religious bullies—cannot be appeased; they have to be opposed with courage, clarity, and conviction. This is never easy. These true believers don't fight fair. Robert's Rules of Order is not one of their holy texts.
- Bill Moyers

Children are still dying at the hands of bullying.
- Marlo Thomas

Bumper Stickers

If corporations are people, arrest them for their crimes
- Bumper sticker

Nice Hummer—Sorry About Your Penis
- Bumper sticker

Evolution Is Just a Theory ... Kind of Like Gravity
- Bumper sticker

My Comedy Channel: Fox News
My News Channel: Comedy Central
- Bumper sticker

Don't pray in my school and I won't think in your church.
- Bumper sticker

If you cut off my reproductive rights, can I cut off yours?
- Bumper sticker

Tea Parties are for little girls with imaginary friends
- Bumper sticker

Dear 1%, We fell asleep for a while.
Just woke up. Sincerely, the other 99%
- Bumper sticker

Human Need Not Corporate Greed
- Bumper sticker

Santorum: Just Google It
- Bumper sticker

Did I Vote on Your Marriage?
- Bumper sticker

Our factories are all overseas. All we produce here are rich
executives.
- Bumper sticker

Campaign Finance

Money! It is money! Money! Money! Not ideas, nor
principles, but money that reigns supreme in American
politics.
- Robert C. Byrd

The principal power in Washington is no longer the
government or the people it represents. It is the Money
Power. Under the deceptive cloak of campaign
contributions, access and influence, votes and
amendments are bought and sold.
- Richard N. Goodwin

Elections are more often bought than won.
- Lee Hamilton

The root, the thing that feeds the other ills, and the thing
that we must kill first.
- Lawrence Lessing, on our corrupt system of campaign
financing

Our President Should Be Elected by Voters, Not Dollars
- Slogan from Public Citizen

There's one word to describe what's going on in the
campaign-finance area: The word is 'obscene.' And it's
going to result in scandal and corruption.
- Fred Wertheimer

Capitalism

Growth for the sake of growth is the ideology of a cancer cell.
- Edward Abbey

Corporate capitalism, if left unchecked, will kill us.
- Chris Hedges

We've seen the results of capitalism without conscience: the pollution of the air we breathe, the water we drink, and the food we eat; the endangerment of workers; and the sales of dangerous products—from cars to toys to drugs. All in pursuit of greater and greater profits.
- Arianna Huffington

Capitalism today commands the towering heights, and has displaced politics and politicians as the new high priests, and reigning oligarchs of our system.
- Ira Jackson

Capitalism is the extraordinary belief that the nastiest of men, for the nastiest of reasons, will somehow work for the benefit of us all.
- John Maynard Keynes

We have deluded ourselves into believing the myth that capitalism grew and prospered out of the Protestant ethic of hard work and sacrifices. Capitalism was built on the exploitation of black slaves and continues to thrive on the exploitation of the poor, both black and white, both here and abroad.
- Martin Luther King

Not every problem someone has with his girlfriend is necessarily due to the capitalist mode of production.
- Herbert Marcuse

The problem with capitalism is that it best rewards the worst part of us: the ruthless, competitive, conniving, opportunistic, acquisitive drives, giving little reward . . . to honesty, compassion, [and] fair play.
- Michael Parenti

Advocates of capitalism are very apt to appeal to the sacred principles of liberty, which are embodied in one maxim: The fortunate must not be restrained in the exercise of tyranny over the unfortunate.
- Bertrand Russell

Capitalism and democracy are incompatible.
- Marina Sitrin

Businesses succeed not through competitive merit but through government connections and favoritism such as tax breaks, subsidies and other preferential treatment.
- Luigi Zingales, defining crony capitalism

Church and State

The United States is not a Christian nation any more than
it is a Jewish or a Mohammedan one.
- John Adams

I'm completely in favor of the separation of Church and
State. My idea is that these two institutions screw us up
enough on their own, so both of them together is certain
death.
- George Carlin

The divorce between Church and State ought to be
absolute. It ought to be so absolute that no Church
property anywhere, in any state or in the nation, should be
exempt from equal taxation; for if you exempt the property
of any church organization, to that extent you impose a tax
upon the whole community.
- James A. Garfield

Secularists are often wrongly accused of trying to purge
religious ideals from public discourse. We simply want to
deny them public sponsorship.
- Wendy Kaminer

Considering the generous tax exemptions long enjoyed by
religious institutions, the routine invocation of God at
official events or even the persistence of blue laws
prohibiting the sale of liquor on Sundays, it's clear that the
"wall" between church and state has never been much
more than a curtain.
- Wendy Kaminer

I believe in an America where the separation of church and
state is absolute.
- John F. Kennedy

Those who would renegotiate the boundaries between church and state must therefore answer a difficult question: why would we trade a system that has served us so well for one that has served others so poorly?
- Sandra Day O'Connor

The word "God" does not appear in the Constitution.
- Arthur Schlesinger

Citizens United v. Federal Election Commission

One of the most lawless decisions in the history of this country and of the Supreme Court. It throws open our political process to huge corporations including foreign money.
- Russell D. Feingold

The Supreme Court in essence has ruled that corporations can buy elections.
- Alan Grayson

Despite nearly 100 years of statutes and precedent that establish the authority of Congress to limit the corrupting influence of corporate money in federal elections, the Court today ruled that corporations are absolutely free to spend shareholder money with the intent to promote the election or defeat of a candidate for political office.
- Edward E. Kaufman

Today's decision . . . will increase the stranglehold corporations now have over politics. There is no more effective way to concentrate even more money and power in the hands of the wealthy.
- Dennis Kucinich

Five Supreme Court justices have struck down the distinction between individuals and corporations in election law and opened the floodgates to a hostile corporate takeover of our democratic process.
- Rosa L. DeLauro

We are rapidly moving toward a nation of the super-rich, by the super-rich and for the super-rich.
- Bernie Sanders

The bottom line is, the Supreme Court has just predetermined the winners of next November's election. It won't be the Republican or the Democrats and it won't be the American people; it will be Corporate America.
- Charles Schumer

I think this is the absolute worst Supreme Court decision in the court's history and should be overturned for many, many reasons, first and foremost because it is a perversion democracy.
- John Paul Stevens, retired Supreme Court Justice

Civil Disobedience

Mass non-violent protest is predicated on the humanity of the oppressor. Quite often it doesn't work.
- Noam Chomsky

Non-cooperation with evil is as much a duty as is cooperation with good.
- Mahatma Gandhi

One has a moral responsibility to disobey unjust laws.
- Martin Luther King

Never doubt that a small group of thoughtful, committed individuals can change the world, indeed it's the only thing that ever has.
- Margaret Meade

I believe that Gandhi was correct. Non-violent civil disobedience is the only way to bring about change that allows people to enjoy the change and not get killed in the process.
- Edward James Olmos

I honestly do not know if civil disobedience has any effect on the government. I can promise you it has a great effect on the person who chooses to do it.
- Martin Sheen

Disobedience, in the eyes of anyone who has read history, is man's original virtue.
- Oscar Wilde

Civil disobedience is not our problem. Our problem is civil obedience. Our problem is that numbers of people all over the world have obeyed the dictates of the leaders of their government and have gone to war, and millions have been killed because of this obedience.
- Howard Zinn

Civil Liberty

Liberty is always unfinished business.
- American Civil Liberties Union

You can protect your liberties in this world only by
protecting the other man's freedom. You can be free only if
I am free.
- Clarence Darrow

The liberties of none are safe unless the liberties of all are
protected.
- William O. Douglas

I believe in the Bill of Rights the way some people believe in
the Bible.
- Molly Ivins

It is possible to read the history of this country as one long
struggle to extend the liberties established in our
Constitution to everyone in America.
- Molly Ivins

Class

There's class warfare, all right, but it's my class, the rich class, that's making war, and we're winning.
- Warren Buffett

Years ago I recognized my kinship with all living beings, and I made up my mind that I was not one bit better than the meanest on earth.
- Eugene V. Debs

While there is a lower class, I am in it, and while there is a criminal element I am of it, and while there is a soul in prison, I am not free.
- Eugene V. Debs

Suffering engenders passion; and while the prosperous blind themselves, or go to sleep, the hatred of the unfortunate classes kindles its torch.
- Victor Hugo

The history of all hitherto existing society is the history of class struggles.
- Karl Marx

The corporate right and the political right declared class warfare on working people a quarter of a century ago and they've won.
- Bill Moyers

Compassion

Compassion brings us to a stop, and for a moment we rise above ourselves.
- Mason Cooley

If you want others to be happy, practice compassion. If you want to be happy, practice compassion.
- Dalai Lama

Compassion is the antitoxin of the soul: where there is compassion even the most poisonous impulses remain relatively harmless.
- Eric Hoffer

At one time, phrases such as Christian charity and Christian tolerance were used to denote kindness and compassion. To perform a "Christian" act meant an act of giving, of acceptance, of toleration. Now, Christian is invariably linked to right-wing conservative political thought.
- Peter McWilliams

And as I've gotten older, I've had more of a tendency to look for people who live by kindness, tolerance, compassion, a gentler way of looking at things.
- Martin Scorsese

I am not interested in picking up crumbs of compassion thrown from the table of someone who considers himself my master. I want the full menu of rights.
- Desmond Tutu

Conformity

The reward for conformity is that everyone likes you but yourself.
- Rita Mae Brown

Our love of lockstep is our greatest curse, the source of all that bedevils us. It is the source of homophobia, xenophobia, racism, sexism, terrorism, [and] bigotry.
- Anna Quindlen

We need more people speaking out. This country is not overrun with rebels and free thinkers. It's overrun with sheep and conformists.
- Bill Maher

As corporations grow larger and advertising grows more sophisticated, culture in general glides more than ever into groupthink.
- Anneli Rufus

A man must consider what a rich realm he abdicates when he becomes a conformist.
- Publilius Syrus

Conservatives

What on Earth did conservatism ever accomplish for our country?
- Charles Kuralt

All conservatives are such from personal defects. They have been effeminated by position or nature, born halt and blind, through luxury of their parents, and can only, like invalids, act on the defensive.
- Ralph Waldo Emerson

All claims of the right . . . advance from victimhood.
- Thomas Frank

A study published in the journal "Psychological Science" showed that children who score low on intelligence tests gravitate toward socially conservative political views in adulthood.
- David Freeman

The modern conservative is engaged in one of man's oldest exercises in moral philosophy; that is, the search for a superior moral justification for selfishness.
- John Kenneth Galbraith

Conservatives have historically seen people falling through the cracks in society and said that's the way things work, survival of the fittest.
- Jim Hightower

[Conservatism] is centrally dependent upon hatred of an Enemy, foreign or domestic – the Terrorist, the Immigrant, the Faggot, and most of all, the Liberal.
- Glen Greenwalt

Remember the whiny, insecure kid in nursery school. The one who always thought everyone was out to get him, and was always running to the teacher with complaints? Chances are he grew up to be conservative.
- Kurt Kliener, from the Journal of Research into Personality

Conservatives . . . seek their self-interest and their own well-being without worrying or being responsible for the well-being or interest of anybody else.
- George Lakoff

If conservatives don't want to be seen as bitter people who cling to their guns and religion and anti-immigrant sentiments, they should stop being bitter and clinging to their guns, religion and anti-immigrant sentiments.
- Bill Maher

The corporate conservatives and their allies in the political and religious right are achieving a vast transformation of American life . . . . They are systematically stripping government of all its functions except rewarding the rich and waging war.
 - Bill Mowers

The central political agenda of America's conservative forces is to protect corporate power.
- Michael Lerner

Please identify one rightwing idea that has moved American society forward.
- Ted Rall

The self-made myth . . . sits at the deep black heart of the entire right-wing worldview.
- Sara Robinson

Corporate Media

The media are corporations, parts of bigger corporations,
they're very closely linked to other systems of power both
in personnel and interests and social background and
everything else. Naturally they tend to be reactionary.
- Noam Chomsky

Conservatives enjoy their virtual monopoly over the
nation's political conversation . . . They paid a lot of money
for it and they intend to keep it.
- Joe Conason

Journalism is the only profession explicitly protected by
the U.S. Constitution, because journalists are supposed to
be the check and balance on government. We're supposed
to be holding those in power accountable. We're not
supposed to be their megaphone. That's what the corporate
media have become.
- Amy Goodman

New Rule: If one of your news organization's headlines is
about who got kicked off Dancing with the Stars last night,
you're no longer a news organization.
- Bill Maher

If you're not careful the media will have you hating the
people who are being oppressed, and loving the people who
are doing the oppressing.
- Malcolm X

The corruption of journalistic integrity is always bad, but it
becomes obscene under conditions of extreme media
concentration as now exist.
- Robert McChesney

The Founders didn't count on the rise of mega-media. They
didn't count on huge private corporations that would own
not only the means of journalism but also vast swaths of
the territory that journalism should be covering.
- Bill Moyers

In America, the arms industry, the oil industry, the major media networks, and, indeed, US foreign policy, are all controlled by the same business combines.
- Arundhati Roy

It is difficult to produce a television documentary that is both incisive and probing when every twelve minutes one is interrupted by twelve dancing rabbits singing about toilet paper.
- Rod Serling

The commercial media are greed-driven enterprises dominated by a dozen transnational companies. Newsroom staffs have been downsized. Much of what you see on national and local TV news is actually video news releases prepared by public-relations firms and given free to TV stations and networks.
- John Stauber

Corporate news media are dependent on public relations. Half of everything in the news actually originates from a PR firm.
- John Stauber

I look at politicians as they are doing what inherently they need to do to retain power. Their job is to consolidate power. When you go to the zoo and you see a monkey throwing poop, you go, "that's what monkeys do, what are you gonna do?" But what I wish the media would do more frequently is say "bad monkey."
- Jon Stewart, on the failure of the news organizations

The corporate grip on opinion in the United States is one of the wonders of the Western world.
- Gore Vidal

Corporate Power

The twentieth century has been characterized by three
developments of great political importance: the growth of
democracy; the growth of corporate power; and the growth
of propaganda as a means of protecting corporate power
against democracy.
- Alex Carey

The biggest threat to American democracy is corporate
power.
- Robert F. Kennedy, Jr.

These bastards who run our country are a bunch of
conniving, thieving, smug pricks who need to be brought
down and removed and replaced with a whole new system
that we control.
- Michael Moore

In our society, corporations and the wealthy enjoy a power
every bit as immense as that assumed to have been
enjoyed by the lords and royalty of feudal times.
- Robert W. McChesney,

Corporations have effectively captured the United States:
its judiciary, its political system, and its national wealth,
without assuming any of the responsibilities of dominion.
Evidence is everywhere.
- Robert A.G. Monks

Our country has far more problems than it deserves and
far more solutions than it applies. The reason: excessive
concentration of power and wealth in a few hands. Instead
of government of, by, and for the people, we have a
government of the Exxons, by the General Motors, and for
the DuPonts.
- Ralph Nader

The history of the twentieth century was dominated by the struggle against totalitarian systems of state power. The twenty-first will no doubt be marked by a struggle to curtail excessive corporate power.
- Eric Schlosser

You have no idea of all the crimes people in business commit every day. Like it was nothing. Or there's a set of special rules for them.
- Andrew Vachss

If those in charge of our society - politicians, corporate executives, and owners of press and television - can dominate our ideas, they will be secure in their power. They will not need soldiers patrolling the streets. We will control ourselves.
- Howard Zinn

Corporations

Why should workers agree to be slaves in a basically authoritarian structure? They should have control over it themselves.
- Noam Chomsky

It more than a little strange to gaze out over a land laid waste by fantastic corporate fraud and declare that partisanship is what ails us and that reasonableness is the cure.
- Thomas Frank, on Jon Stewart's "Rally to Restore Sanity"

The corporation is designed to make money without regard to human life, the social good or impact on the environment.
- Chris Hedges

Corporations have intruded into every facet of life. We eat corporate food. We buy corporate clothes. We drive corporate cars. We buy our vehicular fuel and our heating oil from corporations. We borrow from corporate banks. We invest our retirement savings with corporations... They are vampires.
- Chris Hedges

If some company is too big to fail, then it's too big to exist. Break it up.
- Bob Herbert

The corporations don't have to lobby the government anymore. They are the government.
- Jim Hightower

Corporations put ads on fruit, ads all over the schools, ads on cars, ads on clothes. The only place you can't find ads is where they belong: on politicians.
- Molly Ivins

I hope we shall crush in its birth the aristocracy of our moneyed corporations which dare already to challenge our government to a trial of strength and bid defiance to the laws our country.
- Thomas Jefferson

I see in the near future a crisis approaching that unnerves me and causes me to tremble for the safety of my country . . . corporations have been enthroned and an era of corruption in high places will follow.
- Abraham Lincoln

Today the large organization is lord and master, and most of its employees have been desensitized much as were the medieval peasants who never knew they were serfs.
- Ralph Nader

Corporations are not people. They do not breathe; they do not have children; they do not die fighting in wars for our country. And they do not vote in elections. We need to act to get their money out of our elections.
- C.B. Pearson

They want a docile labor force, disciplined by the fear of job loss, unable to combine with fellow workers for better pay and working conditions.
- Harold Piety

Courage

Have the courage to live. Anyone can die.
- Robert Cody

You can't test courage cautiously.
- Anne Dillard

There is nothing more majestic than the determined
courage of individuals willing to suffer and sacrifice for
their freedom and dignity.
- Martin Luther King

I wanted you to see what real courage is, instead of getting
the idea that courage is a man with a gun in his hand. It's
when you know you're licked before you begin but you
begin anyway and you see it through no matter what.
- Harper Lee

Life shrinks or expands in proportion to one's courage.
- Anais Nin

Courage doesn't always roar. Sometimes courage is the
little voice at the end of the day that says I'll try again
tomorrow.
- Mary Anne Radmacher

It is curious—curious that physical courage should be so
common in the world, and moral courage so rare.
- Mark Twain

Crime and Punishment

Behind every great fortune there is a great crime.
- Honore de Balzac

Great is the mischief of legal crime.
- Ralph Waldo Emerson

America has become a country that imprisons those it fails.
- Beverly Henry

The United States has now become the world leader in its rate of incarceration, locking up its citizens at five to eight times the rate of other industrialized nations.
- Marc Mauer

Who built the moral cesspool into which this nation has sunk with its secret prisons and secret prisoners, legalized torture, indefinite imprisonment without trial or counsel?
- Floyd J. McKay

If we were to judge the US by its penal policies, we would perceive a strange beast: a Christian society that believes in neither forgiveness nor redemption.
- George Monbiot

Distrust all in whom the impulse to punish is powerful.
- Friedrich Nietzsche

Crime is a logical extension of the sort of behavior that is often considered perfectly respectable in legitimate business.
- Robert Rice

A criminal is a person with predatory instincts without sufficient capital to form a corporation.
- Howard Scott

41

[Imprisonment] is a cruel and useless substitute for the elimination of those conditions -- poverty, unemployment, homelessness, desperation, racism, greed -- which are at the root of most punished crime.
- Howard Zinn

The crimes of the rich and powerful go mostly unpunished.
- Howard Zinn

Democracy

We're not a democracy. It's a terrible misunderstanding and a slander to the idea of democracy to call us that. In reality, we're a plutocracy: a government by the wealthy.
- Ramsey Clark, former U.S. Attorney General

The most effective way to restrict democracy is to transfer decision-making from the public arena to unaccountable institutions: kings and princes, priestly castes, military juntas, party dictatorships, or modern corporations.
- Noam Chomsky

I'm in favor of democracy, which means that the central institutions in the society have to be under popular control. Now, under capitalism we can't have democracy by definition. Capitalism is a system in which the central institutions of society are in principle under autocratic control.
- Noam Chomsky

The two greatest obstacles to democracy in the United States are, first, the widespread delusion among the poor that we have a democracy, and second, the chronic terror among the rich, lest we get it.
- Edward Dowling

Democracy is not a spectator sport.
- Marian Wright Edelman

It should be no surprise that when rich men take control of the government, they pass laws that are favorable to themselves. The surprise is that those who are not rich vote for such people, even though they should know from bitter experience that the rich will continue to rip off the rest of us.
- Andrew Greeley

The proper goal of an economic democracy agenda is to replace the global suicide economy ruled by rapacious and unaccountable global corporations.
- David Korten

Man's capacity for justice makes democracy possible, but man's inclination to injustice makes democracy necessary.
- Reinhold Niebuhr

Democracy, the modern world's holy cow, is in crisis. And the crisis is a profound one. Every kind of outrage is being committed in the name of democracy.
- Arundhati Roy

Whenever you find yourself on the side of the majority, it is time to pause and reflect.
- Mark Twain

Dignity

The primal principle of democracy is the worth and dignity of the individual.
- Edward Bellamy

From the depth of need and despair, people can work together, can organize themselves to solve their own problems and fill their own needs with dignity and strength.
- Cesar Chavez

It is the inherent nature of all human beings to yearn for freedom, equality and dignity, and they have an equal right to achieve that.
- Dalai Lama

The ultimate indignity is to be given a bedpan by a stranger who calls you by your first name.
- Maggie Kuhn

You are a human being. You have rights inherent in that reality. You have dignity and worth that exists prior to law.
- Lyn Beth Neylon

When an individual is protesting society's refusal to acknowledge his dignity as a human being, his very act of protest confers dignity on him.
- Bayard Rustin

Our economic and political systems place more value in the accumulation of wealth than in the dignity of people.
- David Taylor

Dissent

The rightful claim to dissent is an existential right of the individual.
- Friedrich Durrenmatt

No matter that patriotism is too often the refuge of scoundrels. Dissent, rebellion, and all-around hell-raising remain the true duty of patriots.
- Barbara Ehrenreich

Human salvation lies in the hands of the creatively maladjusted.
- Martin Luther King

A chill wind s blowing in this nation . . . Every day, the air waves are filled with warnings, veiled and unveiled threats, spewed invective, and hatred directed at any voice of dissent.
- Tim Robbins

Free societies are societies in which the right of dissent is protected.
- Natan Sharansky

If the machine of government is of such a nature that it requires you to be the agent of injustice to another, then, I say, break the law.
- Henry David Thoreau

Dissent is the highest form of patriotism.
- Howard Zinn

Drugs

There still exists on the books a federal death penalty for growing 60,000 marijuana plants.
- Russ Belville

Let's call the drug war what it is – ethnic cleansing of Americans.
- Jello Biafra

One might ask why tobacco is legal and marijuana not. A possible answer is suggested by the nature of the crop. Marijuana can be grown almost anywhere, with little difficulty. It might not be easily marketable by major corporations. Tobacco is quite another story.
- Noam Chomsky

I used to smoke marijuana. But I'll tell you something: I would only smoke it in the late evening. Oh, occasionally the early evening, but usually the late evening - or the mid-evening. Just the early evening, midevening and late evening. Occasionally, early afternoon, early mid-afternoon, or perhaps the late-midafternoon. Oh, sometimes the early-mid-late-early morning. . . But never at dusk! Never at dusk, I would never do that.
- Steve Martin

I'm glad I don't have to explain to a man from Mars why each day I set fire to dozens of little pieces if paper, and then put them in my mouth.
- Mignon McLaughlin

I've never had a problem with drugs. I've had problems with the police.
- Keith Richards

I wouldn't recommend sex, drugs, or insanity for everyone, but they've always worked for me.
- Hunter S. Thompson

Economic Crisis

Can we envision an economy designed to serve the society,
rather than the other way around?
- William Greider

Economics has always been nothing more than politics in
disguise.
- Hazel Henderson

My administration is the only thing between you and the
pitchforks.
- Barack Obama, to bank CEOs

The conduct of America's financial giants amounted to a
frenzy of greed.
- Harold Piety

We must never forget that this economic crisis was caused
by the greed, recklessness and illegal behavior of a handful
of executives on Wall Street.
- Bernie Sanders

While the financial crisis destroyed careers and
reputations, and left many more bruised and battered, it
also left the survivors with a genuine sense of
invulnerability at having made it back from the brink. Still
missing in the current environment is a genuine sense of
humility.
- Andrew Ross Sorkin

In the end, our government had no mechanism for
searching the balance sheets of companies that held life-
or-death power over our society.
- Matt Taibbi

Why has our economic system made the rich richer for
decades while everyone else works harder just to get by?
- Richard Wolff

The way big banks escaped the financial crisis with their profits intact (and often enhanced) epitomized American-style crony capitalism. Neither party has had the courage to confront it, for fear of losing campaign contributions and political power.

- Luigi Zingales

Education

Anyone who believes that children are our future has never been to a mall.
- Andy Borowitz

Mass education was designed to turn independent farmers into docile, passive tools of production. That was its primary purpose.
- Noam Chomsky

If schools were, in reality, democratic, there would be no need to bombard students with platitudes about democracy . . . The more there is a need to talk about the ideals of democracy, the less democratic the system usually is.
- Noam Chomsky

The crippling of individuals I consider the worst evil of capitalism. Our whole educational system suffers from this evil. An exaggerated competitive attitude is inculcated into the student, who is trained to worship acquisitive success as a preparation for his future career.
- Albert Einstein

Only the educated are free.
- Epictetus

Education either functions as an instrument which is used to facilitate integration of the younger generation into the logic of the present system and bring about conformity or it becomes the practice of freedom, the means by which men and women deal critically and creatively with reality and discover how to participate in the transformation of their world.
- Paulo Freire

A liberal education frees a man from the prison-house of his class, race, time, place, background, family, and even nation.
- Robert Maynard Hutchins

The explosion in student debt is a direct outgrowth of the defunding of education in state after state. Unlike corporate and other debt, student debt is excluded from bankruptcy relief, strangling students for life.
- Stephen Lerner

We blame teachers for being unable to cure social ills that no one knows how to treat; we insist that they instantly adopt whatever "solution" has most recently been concocted by our national panacea machine; and in the process, we demoralize, even paralyze, the very teachers who could help us find our way.
- Parker Palmer

It is not enough to simply teach children to read; we have to give them something worth reading.
- Katherine Paterson

The principle goal of education in the schools should be creating men and women who are capable of doing new things, not simply repeating what other generations have done.
- Jean Piaget

It's facile to blame schools and teachers, but more realistic to recognize that poverty is a reflection of economic conditions. Schools cannot create jobs, provide homes for the homeless, or change the economy.
- Diane Ravitch

We are miseducating the young to believe that military heroism is the noblest form of heroism, when it should be remembered only as the tragic accompaniment of horrendous policies driven by power and profit.
- Howard Zinn

Environment

The notion that we can take and take and take and take, waste and waste, without consequences, is driving the biosphere to destruction.
- Ray Anderson

Nature to be commanded, must be obeyed.
- Francis Bacon

The destiny of humans cannot be separated from the destiny of earth.
- Thomas Berry

We cannot go on treating nature like an all-you-can-eat buffet.
- Grethen C. Daily

Nature-Deficit Disorder
- Headline about the increasing disconnect between people and their environment

Everything is connected; nothing is separate.
- P.D. Ouspensky

Plans to protect air and water, wilderness and wildlife are in fact plans to protect man.
- Stewart Udall

I really wonder what gives us the right to wreck this poor planet of ours.
- Kurt Vonnegut

The magnificence of mountains, the serenity of nature - nothing is safe from the idiot marks of man's passing.
- Loudon Wainwright

If we continue felling the forests, polluting the earth, and using up all the water, our grandchildren won't have much of a planet left.
- Chip Ward

Only in the last moment in history has the delusion arisen that people can flourish apart from the rest of the living world.
- E.O. Wilson

Equality

I will not disgrace my religion, my people or myself by
becoming a tool to enslave those who are fighting for their
own justice, freedom and equality.
- Muhammad Ali, on his refusal to be drafted into the
Vietnam War

Political Freedom without economic equality is a pretense,
a fraud, [and] a lie.
- Mikhail Bakunin

We hold these truths to be self-evident, that all Men are
created equal, that they are endowed by their Creator with
certain unalienable Rights, that among these are Life,
Liberty and the Pursuit of Happiness.
- Declaration of Independence

To call woman the weaker sex is a libel; it is man's
injustice to woman.
- Mahatma Gandhi

I don't want to be your other half. I believe that one and
one make two.
- Alanis Morissette

If women are expected to do the same work as men, we
must teach them the same things.
- Plato

Equality of rights under the law shall not be denied or
abridged by the United States or by any state on account of
sex.
- Proposed Equal Rights Amendment not ratified by
enough states and expired in 1982

Just think – guns have a constitutional amendment
protecting them and women don't.
- Eleanor Smeal

I do not wish them [women] to have power over men; but over themselves.
— Mary Wollstonecraft

Virtue can only flourish among equals.
- Mary Wollstonecraft

Evil

Silence is evil's closest ally.
- Gary Amirault

It is only in folk tales, children's stories, and the journals of intellectual opinion that power is used wisely and well to destroy evil. The real world teaches very different lessons, and it takes willful and dedicated ignorance to fail to perceive them.
- Noam Chomsky

To ignore evil is to become an accomplice to it.
- Martin Luther King

Men never do evil so completely and cheerfully as when they do it from religious conviction.
- Blaise Pascal

The price of apathy in public affairs is to be ruled by evil men.
- Plato

Evolution and Creationism

Creationists make it sound as though a "theory" is
something you dreamt up after being drunk all night.
- Isaac Asimov

The proper place for the study of religious beliefs is in a
church or temple, at home, or in a course on comparative
religions, but not in a biology class.
- Tim Berra

We have fossils... We win!
- Lewis Black

I would defend the liberty of consenting adult creationists
to practice whatever intellectual perversions they like in
the privacy of their own homes; but it is also necessary to
protect the young and innocent.
- Arthur C. Clarke

If I were a religious person, I would consider creationism
nothing less than blasphemy. Do its adherents imagine
that God is a cosmic hoaxer who has created that whole
vast fossil record for the sole purpose of misleading
mankind?
- Arthur C. Clarke

There is no "Complete Idiots Guide to Creationism," but
perhaps one is not needed.
- Andrei Codrescu

Evolution does not require the nonexistence of God, it
merely allows for it.
- Keith Doyle

If we are going to teach "creation science" as an alternative
to evolution, then we should also teach the stork theory as
an alternative to biological reproduction.
- Judith Hayes

Science has proof without any certainty. Creationists have certainty without any proof.
- Ashley Montague

Faith

I feel no need for any other faith than my faith in human beings.
- Pearl S. Buck

Faith isn't believing without proof – it's trusting without reservation.
- William Sloane Coffin

I've never understood how God could expect His creatures to pick the one true religion by faith—it strikes me as a sloppy way to run a universe.
- Robert A. Heinlein

It is important to have faith, but not necessarily in God. Faith is important far beyond religion: having faith in oneself, in other people, in the existence of truth and justice.
- Tor Norretranders

Fascism

[Fascism is] a system of government that exercises a dictatorship of the extreme right, typically through the merging of state and business leadership, together with belligerent nationalism.
- American Heritage Dictionary

Fascist and proto-fascist regimes were never proclaimed as godless by their opponents. In fact, most of the regimes attached themselves to the predominant religion of the country and chose to portray themselves as militant defenders of that religion.
- Lawrence Britt

A corporation or an industry is, if we were to think of it in political terms, fascist; that is, it has tight control at the top and strict obedience has to be established at every level -- there's a little bargaining, a little give and take, but the line of authority is perfectly straightforward.
- Noam Chomsky

Fascists strut, while conservatives lounge.
- Terry Eagelton

Fascism is the control of government by business.
- Robert F. Kennedy, Jr.

When fascism comes to America, it will be wrapped in the flag and carrying the cross.
- Sinclair Lewis

I think one of the greatest untold stories of the 20th century is the collusion between corporations, especially in America, and Nazi Germany.
- Michael Moore

The liberty of a democracy is not safe if the people tolerate the growth of private power to a point where it becomes stronger than their democratic state itself. That, in its essence, is fascism.
- Franklin Delano Roosevelt

Fascism is capitalism plus murder.
- Upton Sinclair

That which the fascists hate, above all else, is intelligence.
- Miguel de Unamuno

Feminism

There is a special place in hell for women who do not help other women.
- Madeleine K. Albright

Feminism is an entire worldview or gestalt, not just a laundry list of women's issues.
- Charlotte Bunch

We need a kind of feminism that aims not just to assimilate into the institutions that men have created over the centuries, but to infiltrate and subvert them.
- Barbara Ehrenreich

Who knows what women can be when they are finally free to become themselves?
- Betty Friedan

You can't call yourself a feminist if you don't believe in the right to abortion.
- Nora Ephron

Women are the only exploited group in history to have been idealized into powerlessness.
- Erica Jong

Patriarchy is a system in which both women and men participate. It privileges . . . the interests of boys and men over the bodily integrity, autonomy, and dignity of girls and women. It is subtle, insidious, and never more dangerous than when women passionately deny that they themselves are engaging in it.
- Ashley Judd

Feminism is the radical notion that women are people.
- Cheris Kramarae and Paula Treichler

Any woman that tells the truth about herself is a feminist.
- Alice Munro

Women have learned to describe everything they do, no matter how apparently conformist, submissive, self-destructive or humiliating, as a personal choice that cannot be criticized because personal choice is what feminism is all about.
- Katha Pollitt

Ain't she sweet; making profits off her meat.
- Protest sign at Miss America beauty pageant

People call me a feminist whenever I express sentiments that differentiate me from a doormat or a prostitute.
- Rebecca West

Fox News

FAUX News Channel
- Bumper sticker

FOX News: Rich people paying rich people to tell middle
class people to blame poor people
- Bumper sticker

CBS News today has fired four employees for wildly
fabricating a news story. The good news: they all got jobs
over at Fox.
- Craig Ferguson

Another study has concluded that people who only watch
Fox News are less informed than all other news consumers.
- Huffington Post, reporting on research done at Fairleigh
Dickinson University

I have the feeling that about 60 percent of what you say is
crap.
- David Letterman, to Fox News's Bill O'Reilly

[Fox News is] a relentless agenda-driven 24 hours news
opinion propaganda delivery system.
- Jon Stewart

Here's the detail I found most interesting: all the television
sets must be tuned to Fox News.
- Jon Stewart, on Dick Cheney's hotel suite demands

Freedom

I wish that every human life might be pure transparent freedom.
- Simone de Beauvoir

Freedom is nothing else but a chance to be better.
- Albert Camus

I call that mind free which protects itself against the usurpations of society, and which does not cower to human opinion: Which refuses to be the slave or tool of the many or of the few, and guards its empire over itself as nobler than the empire of the world.
- William Ellery Channing

If we don't believe in free expression for people we despise, we don't believe in it at all.
- Noam Chomsky

What man wants is simply independent choice, whatever that independence may cost and wherever it may lead.
- Fyodor Dostoevsky

None are more hopelessly enslaved than those who falsely believe they are free.
- Johann Wolfgang von Goethe

Freedom is never voluntarily given by the oppressor; it must be demanded by the oppressed.
- Martin Luther King

Man is condemned to be free; because once thrown into the world, he is responsible for everything he does.
- Jean-Paul Sartre

My definition of a free society is a society where it is safe to be unpopular.
- Adlai Stevenson

Gay Marriage

Hiding behind religion does not excuse bigotry.
- Ron Chusid

A Senate committee on Thursday approved a constitutional amendment banning same sex marriage, apparently forgetting that our forefathers wore wigs and satin Capri pants.
- Tina Fey

I wonder what percentage of people who are opposed to gay marriage because it doesn't "respect the sanctity of marriage" are divorced?
- Dylan Gallucci

With Dicks in, all 6 WA congressional Democrats favor repeal of gay-marriage ban
- Headline in Seattle Times, referring to Rep. Norm Dicks

Gay marriage won't lead to dog marriage. It is not a slippery slope to rampant inter-species coupling. When women got the right to vote, it didn't lead to hamsters voting.
- Bill Maher

Gays and lesbians and transgender persons are our brothers, our sisters, our children, our cousins, our friends, our co-workers, and they've got to be treated like every other American.
- Barack Obama

Love and commitment are rare enough; it seems absurd to thwart them in any guise.
- Anna Quindlen

Global Warming

Here is the truth: The Earth is round; Saddam Hussein did not attack us on 9/11; Elvis is dead; Obama was born in the United States; and the climate crisis is real.
- Al Gore

The insistence on complete certainty about the full details of global warming - the most serious threat we have ever faced - is actually an effort to avoid facing the awful, uncomfortable truth: that we must act boldly, decisively, comprehensively, and quickly, even before we know every last detail about the crisis.
- Al Gore

If you look at the science about what is happening on Earth and aren't pessimistic, you don't understand the data.
- Paul Hawken

The danger is that global warming may become self-sustaining, if it has not done so already . . . We have to reverse global warming urgently, if we still can.
- Stephen Hawking

People tend to focus on the here and now. The problem is that, once global warming is something that most people can feel in the course of their daily lives, it will be too late to prevent much larger, potentially catastrophic changes.
- Elizabeth Kolbert

Globalization

The greatest weapon of mass destruction is corporate economic globalization.
- Kenny Ausubel

The dominant propaganda systems have appropriated the term "globalization" . . . which privileges the rights of investors and lenders, those of people being incidental.
- Noam Chomsky

War and Globalization go hand in hand. Wall Street, the oil companies and the defense contractors have concurrent and overlapping interests.
- Michel Chossudovsky

We have a global economy that is not structured around democratizing and including people in the decision-making. It's operated in secret.
- Kevin Danaher

We see an increasingly weaker labor movement . . . as a result of the globalization of capital.
- Angela Davis

Globally . . . the unfettered appetites of capitalism have created an intolerable human condition.
- Tom Hayden

The standardization of world culture, with local popular or traditional forms driven out or dumbed down to make way for American television, American music, food, clothes and films, has been seen by many as the very heart of globalization.
- Fredric Jameson

Giant corporations roam the Earth, pitting societies against one another in search of the lowest costs from serf labor and other exactions from authoritarian regimes while pulling down standards of living in more democratic countries.
- Ralph Nader

The essence of globalization is a subordination of human rights, of labor rights, consumer, environmental rights, democracy rights, to the imperatives of global trade and investment.
- Ralph Nader

The only thing worth globalizing is dissent.
- Arundhati Roy

God

If it turns out that there is a God, I don't think that he's evil. But the worst that you can say about him is that basically he's an underachiever.
- Woody Allen

If the concept of God has any validity or use, it can only be to make us larger, freer, and more loving. If God cannot do this, then it is time we got rid of him.
- James Baldwin

The God of the Old Testament is arguably the most unpleasant character in all fiction.
- Richard Dawkins

Either God wants to abolish evil, and cannot; or he can, but does not want to.
- Epicurus

Don't make me come down there.
- God

Let's face it; God has a big ego problem. Why do we always have to worship him?
- Bill Maher

Conscience is God's presence in man.
- Emanuel Swedenborg

A blank page is God's way of showing you how hard it is to be God.
- Unknown

If God created us in his own image, we have more than reciprocated.
- Voltaire

GOP

The GOP is the true party of diversity! There's the ... Far Right, Hard Right, Extreme Right, Ultra Right, Radical Right, Fringe Right, Religious Right, Severely Right, and Kidnapped-Probed-By-Aliens Right.
- Pat Bagley

The GOP has defined itself indelibly as the party of moneyed greed and unfettered imperialism.
- Robert Scheer

You have to wonder how it is that the party the Creationists call home is so Darwinian!
- Jon Stewart

There is a moral crisis in this country. A horrifyingly, back-breaking, bankrupt-the-core-of-this-nation style crisis. But it isn't women or the poor or the middle class or the gay community or health-care advocates or environmentalists that are causing it. It's you.
- Katrina vanden Heuvel, to GOP

71

Greed

Shame on the CEOs who make eight-figure incomes while their lowest-paid employees trudge between food banks.
- Barbara Ehrenreich

Even in a time of elephantine vanity and greed, one never has to look far to see the campfires of gentle people.
- Garrison Keillor

When we have provided against cold, hunger and thirst, all the rest is but vanity and excess.
- Seneca

The original sin of Republicanism is greed.
- John Scalzi

It is preoccupation with possessions, more than anything else, that prevents us from living freely and nobly.
- Henry David Thoreau

We face not a clash between cultures or between red and blue states in this nation, but a clash between justice and greed.
- Jim Winkler

You can't have everything. Where would you put it?
- Steven Wright

Guns

We have cracked down on library books, cell phone calls, fertilizer purchases and wearing shoes in the airport, but we have done almost nothing at the state level to make it harder for either a terrorist, garden variety armed robber, or young person to get their hands on a handgun.
- Sarah Brady

More teenagers die of gunshot wounds than of all natural diseases combined.
- Center for Disease Control and Prevention

The "Stand Your Ground" law is a license to kill.
- Kendall Coffey

In Washington, officials from the National Rifle Association met with a group of high school students. There were no survivors.
- Tina Fey

There is no way to overstate the horror of gun violence in America. Roughly 16,000 to 17,000 Americans are murdered every year.
- Bob Herbert

I am not anti-gun. I'm pro-knife. Consider the merits of the knife. In the first place, you have to catch up with someone in order to stab him . . . Plus, knives don't ricochet. And people are seldom killed while cleaning their knives.
- Molly Ivins

You know what they cannot keep on the shelves in America? Guns, and ammo. Even though Obama and every other pussy Democrat has never even mentioned the issue, these people are ... sure that he and his Negro army are coming for their guns.
- Bill Maher

My view of guns is simple. I hate guns and I cannot imagine why anyone would want to own one. If I had my way, guns for sport would be registered, and all other guns would be banned.
- Deborah Prothrow-Stith, Dean of Harvard School of Public Health

Happiness

It's never too late to have a happy childhood.
- Berke Breathed

People take different roads seeking fulfillment and happiness. Just because they're not on your road doesn't mean they've gotten lost.
- H. Jackson Brown

In the depth of winter I finally learned that there was in me an invincible summer.
- Albert Camus

Happiness is when what you think, what you say, and what you do are in harmony.
- Mahatma Gandhi

Many persons have a wrong idea of what constitutes true happiness. It is not attained through self-gratification but through fidelity to a worthy purpose.
- Helen Keller

Loving your work (unfortunately the privilege of the few) represents the best, most concrete approximation of happiness on earth.
- Primo Levi

Happiness is not a goal; it is a by-product.
- Eleanor Roosevelt

Health Care

Republican talking point: Under Obamacare, to qualify for benefits you will be forced to smoke medical marijuana until you are gay.
- Andy Borowitz

Trump Says John Roberts' Birth Certificate is Fake
- Andy Borowitz, after the chief justice declared Obamacare to be constitutional

No one should have to choose between medicine and other necessities. No one should have to use the emergency room every time a child gets sick. And no one should have to live in constant fear that a medical problem will become a financial crisis.
- Brad Henry

The Republicans, for their part, have accepted the decision and said they're going to focus on working with the president. I'm joking, of course. They threw a tantrum, shit in their pants, and flung their feces at the White House.
- Bill Maher, on hearing that Obamacare is constitutional

If it's any consolation [to conservatives], the thieves who run the health insurance companies will still get to deny coverage to adults with pre-existing conditions for the next four years.
- Michael Moore, on the phasing in of Obamacare

We are the richest country in the world. We spend more on health care than any other country. Yet we have the worst health care in the Western world. Come on. We can do better than this.
- Michael Moore

I am not the first President to take up this cause, but I am determined to be the last.
- Barack Obama, health care speech to a joint session of Congress

The only health care mandate they can embrace are transvaginal probes for women.
- Martin O'Malley, on Republican hypocrisy

Homelessness

You can spend the money on new housing for poor people and the homeless, or you can spend it on a football stadium or a golf course.
- Jello Biafra

The baby Jesus was the last homeless person the Republicans liked.
- Andy Borowitz

When I was living in New York and didn't have a penny to my name, I would walk around the streets and occasionally I would see an alcove or something. And I'd think, that'll be good, that'll be a good spot for me when I'm homeless.
- Larry David

What difference does it make to the dead, the orphans, and the homeless, whether the mad destruction is wrought under the name of totalitarianism or the holy name of liberty or democracy?
- Mohandas Gandhi

The wretched refuse of your teeming shore. Send these, the homeless, tempest-tost to me, I lift my lamp beside the golden door
 - Emma Lazarus, from her sonnet inscribed on the Statue of Liberty

Seven out of 10 Americans are one paycheck away from being homeless.
- Pras Michel

How can we worship a homeless Man on Sunday and ignore one on Monday?
- Unknown

All these people talking about morality should just take a walk downtown. They don't want to go downtown because instantly they see homeless people and they don't want to.
- Neil Young

Homophobia

Homophobia is apparently associated with homosexual arousal that the homosexual individual is either unaware of or denies.
- H. E. Adams, *Journal of Abnormal Psychology*

The only queer people are those who don't love anybody.
- Rita Mae Brown

There are more scriptural reasons to oppose homophobia than to oppose homosexuality.
- Rev. John B. Cobb

For Christians, the problem is not how to reconcile homosexuality with scriptural passages that condemn it, but how to reconcile the rejection and punishment of homosexuals with the love of Christ.
- Rev. William Sloane Coffin

Homosexuality is found in over 450 species. Homophobia is found in only one.
- Protest sign

Hope

The grand essentials to happiness in this life are something to do, something to love, and something to hope for.
- Joseph Addison

Make no little plans; they have no magic to stir men's blood. Make big plans; aim high in hope and work.
- Daniel Hudson Burnham

Hope is a good thing, maybe the best of things, and no good thing ever dies.
- Stephen King

Another world is not only possible, she is on her way. On a quiet day, I can hear her breathing.
- Arundhati Roy

To be hopeful in bad times is not just foolishly romantic. It is based on the fact that human history is a history not only of cruelty, but also of compassion, sacrifice, courage, [and] kindness.
- Howard Zinn

QUOTES from the UNDERGROUND

Human Nature

We are all in the same boat, in a stormy sea, and we owe
each other a terrible loyalty.
- G.K. Chesterton

When ... in the course of all these thousands of years has
man ever acted in accordance with his own interests?
- Fyodor Dostoevsky

With numbing regularity good people were seen to knuckle
under the demands of authority and perform actions that
were callous and severe.
- Stanley Milgram, social psychologist who conducted
obedience to authority studies

Men have become the tools of their tools.
- Henry David Thoreau

Human beings are not machines, and however powerful
the pressure to conform, they sometimes are so moved by
what they see as injustice that they dare to declare their
independence. In that historical possibility lies hope.
- Howard Zinn

Human Rights

The quest for freedom, dignity, and the rights of man will
never end.
- William J. Brennan

I passionately believe in the power of human rights as a set
of global values to bring our fractured and divided world
together.
- Irene Khan

Whenever there is a conflict between human rights and
property rights, human rights must prevail.
- Abraham Lincoln

Human rights rest on human dignity. The dignity of man is
an ideal worth fighting for and worth dying for.
- Robert Maynard

Human rights is not a religious idea. It is a secular idea,
the product of the last four centuries of Western history.
- Arthur Schlesinger

People everywhere have the same right to life, liberty, and
the pursuit of happiness.
- Howard Zinn

Immigration

The immigration problem was one of our own making, initiated by corporate agribusiness's decades-old mania for a slave-labor force.
- A.V. Krebs

If capital is going to freely cross borders, should people and labor be able to do so as well, going where globalization takes the jobs?
- George Lakoff

Give me your tired, your poor, your huddled masses yearning to be free.
- Emma Lazarus, from her sonnet at the base of the Statue of Liberty

Mitt Romney said Obama is ignoring the real issues with illegals, which is that they keep blowing the grass clippings into his pool.
- Bill Maher

Immigrants want the same things most Americans do: decent jobs, basic rights, and a life free of violence and coercion.
- David Segal

I think we ought to send every illegal back. But instead of starting with the newest arrivals, I think we should start with the ones that have been here illegally the longest. . . . So, it's about time we threw those English bastards out.
- Cenk Uygur

Imperialism

The conquest of the earth, which mostly means the taking it away from those who have a different complexion or slightly flatter noses than ourselves, is not a pretty thing.
- Joseph Conrad

What do nations care about the cost of war, if by spending a few hundred millions in steel and gunpowder they can gain a thousand millions in diamonds and cocoa?
- W.E.B. DuBois

In the councils of government, we must guard against the acquisition of unwarranted influence, whether sought or unsought, by the military industrial complex.
- Dwight D. Eisenhower

We Americans have no commission from God to Police the world.
- Benjamin Harrison

We have to constantly critique imperialist white supremacist patriarchal culture because it is normalized by mass media and rendered unproblematic.
- bell hooks

The arrogance and brutality of empire are not repealed when they temporarily get deployed in a just cause.
- Michael Kazin

Afghanistan—where empires go to die.
- Mike Malloy

This great and powerful force - the accumulated wealth of the United States - has taken over all the functions of Government, Congress, the issue of money, and banking and the army and navy in order to have a band of mercenaries to do their bidding and protect their stolen property.
- Sen. Richard Pettigrew

Every empire . . . tells itself and the world that it is unlike all other empires, that its mission is not to plunder and control but to educate and liberate.
- Edward W. Said

It is in the nature of imperialism that citizens of the imperial power are always among the last to know - or care - about circumstances in the colonies.
- Bertrand Russell

Individuality

I think everybody's weird. We should all celebrate our individuality and not be embarrassed or ashamed of it.
- Johnny Depp

To be yourself in a world that is constantly trying to make you something else is the greatest accomplishment.
- Ralph Waldo Emerson

Taking into account the public's regrettable lack of taste, it is incumbent upon you not to fit in.
- Janeane Garofalo

Care about people's approval and you will be their prisoner.
- Lao Tzu

Remember always that you not only have the right to be an individual, you have an obligation to be one.
- Eleanor Roosevelt

Forgive him, for he believes that the customs of his tribe are the laws of nature.
- George Bernard Shaw

Internet

As the most participatory form of mass speech yet developed, the Internet deserves the highest protection from government intrusion.
- Stewart Dalzell

The greatest thing about the Internet is that you can quote something and just totally make up the source.
- Benjamin Franklin

Five years ago, we thought of the Web as a new medium, not a new economy.
- Clement Mok

The trouble with the Internet is that it's replacing masturbation as a leisure activity.
- Patrick Murray

The Internet – last refuge of the liberal.
- Ernest Partridge

The Internet is the first thing that humanity has built that humanity doesn't understand, the largest experiment in anarchy that we have ever had.
- Eric Schmidt

The Internet isn't free. It just has an economy that makes no sense to capitalism.
- Brad Shapcott

We've all heard that a million monkeys banging on a million typewriters will eventually reproduce the entire works of Shakespeare. Now, thanks to the Internet, we know this is not true.
- Robert Wilensky

Jesus

If this is going to be a Christian nation that doesn't help
the poor, either we have to pretend that Jesus was just as
selfish as we are, or we've got to acknowledge that He
commanded us to love the poor and serve the needy
without condition and then admit that we just don't want
to do it.
- Stephen Corbert

You are free to believe that salvation comes only through
faith in Jesus Christ and to order your behavior
accordingly. You are not free to coerce others, either by
physical force or the force of law, to share your faith and
behave as you do.
- Stanley Fish

Jesus was the first socialist, the first to seek a better life
for mankind.
- Mikhail Gorbachev

The notion that faith in Christ is to be rewarded by an
eternity of bliss, while a dependence upon reason,
observation, and experience merits everlasting pain, is too
absurd for refutation.
- Robert Ingersoll

Jesus in the Gospels repeatedly talks about poverty and
social justice, yet never explicitly mentions either abortion
or homosexuality.
- Nicholas Kristof

I believe that Jesus was a religious liberal . . . Instead of an
eye for an eye, he asked for us to turn the other cheek.
Instead of just loving our neighbors, we were called upon to
love our enemies, too.
- Scotty McLennan

Jesus would Occupy.
- Alan Minsky, on a movement committed to helping the
poor

Jesus . . . was out there fighting injustice and speaking truth to power every single day. He was out there spreading a message of grace and redemption to the least, the last, and the lost. And our charge is to find Him everywhere, every day by how we live our lives.
- Michele Obama

Justice

Equal pay for women is a matter of simple justice.
- Mary Anderson

Laws are spider webs through which the big flies pass and the little ones get caught.
- Honoré de Balzac

The arc of the moral universe is long but it bends towards justice.
- Martin Luther King

It is better to risk saving a guilty man than to condemn an innocent one.
- Voltaire

There may be times when we are powerless to prevent injustice, but there must never be a time when we fail to protest.
- Elie Weisel

Kindness

No act of kindness, however small, is ever wasted.
- Aesop

How far you go in life depends on your being tender with
the young, compassionate with the aged, sympathetic with
the striving, and tolerant of the weak and the strong.
Because someday in life you will have been all of these.
- George Washington Carver

There is no such thing as other people's children.
- Hilary Clinton

Tenderness and kindness are not signs of weakness and
despair, but manifestations of strength and resolution.
- Kahlil Gibran

Three things in human life are important: the first is to be
kind; the second is to be kind; and the third is to be kind.
- Henry James

Small deeds done are better than great deeds planned.
- Peter Marshall

Be kind, for everyone you meet is fighting a great battle.
- Philo of Alexandria

The Left

Don't you see the rest of the country looks upon New York like we're leftwing, communist, Jewish, homosexual pornographers? I think of us that way sometimes and I live here.
- Woody Allen, in Annie Hall

While leftists sit around congratulating themselves on their personal virtue, the right understands the central significance of movement building, and they have taken to the task with admirable diligence.
- Thomas Frank

We forget sometimes that the values we treasure—equality, fairness, justice, dignity, and ultimately kindness and love —inspired the greatest moral and political achievements of the 20th century: civil rights, women's equality, the right to organize, and the growth of the environmental movement.
- Don Hazen

Instead of a left, America has a right wing that has proven powerful enough to pull both major parties significantly in its direction over the past twenty years.
- Mark Hertzgaard

A progressive believes that society can be made . . . "better" only when it's better for everybody.
- Garret Keizer

The six modes of progressive thought: (1) socioeconomic, (2) identity politics, (3) environmentalists, (4) civil libertarians, (5) spiritual, and (6) antiauthoritarian.
- George Lakoff

Be ashamed to die till you have won some victory for humanity.
- Horance Mann

It's the spirit of fighting back throughout American history that brought an end to sweatshops, won the eight-hour working day and a minimum wage, delivered suffrage to women and blacks from slavery, inspired the Gay Rights movement, [and] the consumer and environmental movements.
- Bill Moyers

Many little lefts.
- James Weinstein, on the fragmented, single-issue nature of the American Left

LGBT

The male party line concerning Lesbians is that women become Lesbians out of reaction to men. This is a pathetic illustration of the male ego's inflated proportions. I became a Lesbian because of women.
- Rita Mae Brown

Gay people don't actually try to convert people. That's Jehovah's Witnesses you're thinking of.
- Tina Fey

There is no wholly masculine man, no purely feminine woman.
- Margaret Fuller

Let's make a law that gay people can have birthdays, but straight people get more cake -- you know, to send the right message to kids.
- Bill Maher

Human beings do not choose their sexual orientation; they discover it as something given. To pray for a change in sexual orientation is about as meaningful as to pray for a change from blue eyes to brown.
- John J. McNeill

And the day came when the risk it took to remain closed in a bud became more painful than the risk it took to blossom.
- Anais Nin

If homosexuality is a disease, let's all call in queer to work. "Hello, can't work today, still queer.
- Robin Tyler

Liberal Vice

Economic liberalism is on life-support, while cultural liberalism thrives. The obvious question is why. The simple answer is that cultural liberalism ... does not cost the wealthy anything.
- Eric Alterman

Liberals . . . talk about peace and do nothing to challenge our permanent war economy. They claim to support the working class, and vote for candidates that glibly defend the North American Free Trade Agreement. They insist they believe in welfare, the right to organize, universal health care and a host of other socially progressive causes, and will not risk stepping out of the mainstream to fight for them.
- Chris Hedges

Liberal: a power worshipper without power.
- George Orwell

The object of liberalism has never been to destroy capitalism . . . only to keep the capitalists from destroying it.
- Arthur M. Schlesinger

There is an astonishing lack of anger among liberals, progressives and radicals who have abandoned emotion to the right.
- Clancy Sigal

Why is it that right-wing bastards always stand shoulder to shoulder in solidarity, while liberals fall out among themselves?
- Yevgeny Yevtushenko

Liberal Virtue

Liberalism is secular Christianity.
- Anonymous

A liberal is a man or a woman or a child who looks forward
to a better day, a more tranquil night, and a bright, infinite
future.
- Leonard Bernstein

Reality has a well-known liberal bias.
- Stephen Colbert

Liberals stand for tolerance, magnanimity, community
spirit, the defense of the weak against the powerful, love of
learning, freedom of belief, art and poetry, city life, the very
things that make America worth dying for.
- Garrison Keillor

Liberals believe that we are better off when we live for each
other than when we only live for ourselves.
- Justin Krebs

Hardworking liberals fought the goon squads and won
workers' rights: the eight-hour day, the weekend, health
plans, and pensions.
- George Lakoff

The truth is, most of the good things about this country
have been fought for by liberals. If conservatives had
carried the day, blacks would still be in the back of the
bus, women would be barefoot and pregnant, medical care
would be on a cash-only basis, there'd be mouse feet in
your breakfast cereal and workers would still be sleeping
next to their machines."
- Katha Pollitt

To wear the label [liberal] today seems like an act of
defiance, much as members of the gay rights community
appropriated, from their antagonists, the epithet "queer."
- Jeff Shesol

A liberal holds that he is true to the republic when he is true to himself.
- E.B. White

Living

Do every act of your life as if it were your last.
- Marcus Aurelius

Life may have no meaning. Or even worse, it may have a meaning of which I disapprove.
- Ashleigh Brillant

We must be willing to get rid of the life we've planned, so as to have the life that is waiting for us.
- Joseph Campbell

Life is the sum of your choices.
- Albert Camus

He who isn't busy being born is busy dying.
- Bob Dylan

It is never too late to be what you might have been.
- George Eliot

The chief event of life is the day in which we have encountered a mind that startled us.
- Ralph Waldo Emerson

When I let go of what I am, I become what I might be.
- Lao Tzu

You wanna fly, you got to give up the shit that weighs you down.
- Toni Morrison

The purpose of life ... is to live it, to taste experience to the utmost, to reach out eagerly and without fear for newer and richer experience.
- Eleanor Roosevelt

Know yourself, so that you may live that life peculiar to you, the one and only life you were born to live.
- George Sheehan

The mass of men lead lives of quiet desperation.
- Henry David Thoreau

Love

Love is an act of sedition, a revolt against reason, an uprising in the body politic, a private mutiny.
- Diane Ackerman

Love, by its very nature, is . . .perhaps the most powerful of all anti-political human forces.
- Hannah Arendt

I believe that the world was created and approved by love, that it subsists, coheres, and endures by love, and that, insofar as it is redeemable, it can be redeemed only by love.
- Wendell Berry

Love is patient and kind; love does not envy or boast; it is not arrogant or rude. It does not insist on its own way; it is not irritable or resentful; it does not rejoice at wrongdoing, but rejoices with the truth. Love bears all things, believes all things, hopes all things, endures all things.
- 1 Corinthians 13:4-7

There are people who take the heart out of you, and people who put it back.
- Elizabeth Davis

We are shaped and guided by what we love.
- Johann von Goethe

Man has conquered whole nations, but all his armies could not conquer love.
- Emma Goldman

Do you want me to tell you something really subversive? Love is everything it's cracked up to be . . . It really is worth fighting for, being brave for, risking everything for.
- Erica Jong

The power of love upsets the order of things.
- Genesis Rabbah

That's what careless words do. They make people love you
a little less.
- Arundhati Roy

The world moves for love. It kneels before it in awe.
- M. Night Shyamalan, from "The Village"

I believe that we are all called to stand on the side of love.
- William Sinkford

The first duty of love is to listen.
- Paul Tillich

Markets

Markets . . . drive people to a conception of themselves and society in which you're only after your own good, not the good of others and that's extremely harmful.
- Noam Chomsky

Economists have provided capitalists with a comforting concept called the "free market." . . . It's a mantra conveniently invoked when it is proposed that government do something the faithful don't like, and just as conveniently ignored whenever they want government to do something for them.
- Edward S. Herman

The term "free market" is really a euphemism. What the far right actually means by this term is "lawless market." In a lawless market, entrepreneurs can get away with privatizing the benefits of the market (profits), while socializing its costs (like pollution).
- Steve Kangas

Anyone who honestly believes that low taxes and unfettered free markets are always best should consider moving to Pakistan's tribal areas. They are a triumph of limited government.
- Nickolas Kristof

The notion of the free market is a myth. All markets are shaped by laws and regulations, and unfortunately our laws and regulations are shaped in order to create more inequality and less opportunity.
- Joseph Stiglitz

Materialism

Money is a great servant but a bad master.
- Francis Bacon

He will always be a slave who does not know how to live upon a little.
- Horace

We live in a culture that produces books like "God Wants You to Be Rich" and "Jesus, CEO."
- Molly Ivins

Oh Lord, won't you buy me a Mercedes Benz?
- Janis Joplin

This focus on money and power may do wonders in the marketplace, but it creates a tremendous crisis in our society. People who have spent all day learning how to sell themselves and to manipulate others are in no position to form lasting friendships or intimate relationships.
- Michael Lerner

Beauty is everywhere, love is endless, and joy bleeds from our everyday existence . . .The only thing I can ask of you is to stay free of materialism.
- Dominic Owen Mallary

It is the preoccupation with possessions, more than anything else that prevents us from living freely and nobly.
- Bertrand Russell

It is not the man who has too little who is poor, but the one who craves more.
- Seneca

An attitude to life which seeks fulfillment in the single-minded pursuit of wealth - in short, materialism - does not fit into this world, because it contains within itself no limiting principle, while the environment in which it is placed is strictly limited.
- E.F. Schumacher

Our economy is based on spending billions to persuade people that happiness is buying things.
- Philip Slater

There really are some things that money can't buy.
- Mark E. Smith

Cultivate poverty like a garden herb, like sage. Do not trouble yourself much to get new things . . . Sell your clothes and keep your thoughts.
- Henry David Thoreau

The man is richest whose pleasures are cheapest.
- Henry David Thoreau

Men and Women

I married beneath me. All women do.
- Lady Nancy Astor

You know, men and women are a lot alike in certain situations. Like when they're both on fire – they're exactly alike.
- Dave Attell

If a woman has to choose between catching a fly ball and saving an infant's life, she will choose to save the infant's life without even considering if there are men on base.
- Dave Barry

One is not born a woman, but rather becomes one.
- Simone de Beauvoir

When women are depressed, they eat or go shopping. Men invade another country. It's a whole different way of thinking.
- Elayne Boosler

I will always love the false image I had of you.
- Ashleigh Brilliant

Relationships are hard. It's like a full time job, and we should treat it like one. If your boyfriend or girlfriend wants to leave you, they should give you two weeks' notice. There should be severance pay, the day before they leave you, they should have to find you a temp.
- Bob Ettinger

Sometimes I wonder if men and women really suit each other. Perhaps they should live next door and just visit now and then.
- Katharine Hepburn

Women who seek to be equal with men lack ambition.
- Timothy Leary

We have to believe that man first walked upright to free his hands for masturbation.
- Lily Tomlin

The clearest explanation for the failure of any marriage is that the two people are incompatible; that is, that one is male and the other female.
- Anna Quindlen

Why are women . . . so much more interesting to men than men are to women?"
- Virginia Woolf

Morality

Waste no more time arguing what a good man should be. Be one.
- Marcus Aurelius

I was raised the old-fashioned way, with a stern set of moral principles: Never lie, cheat, steal, or knowingly spread a venereal disease.
- Barbara Ehrenreich

Things that will destroy man: Politics without principle; pleasure without conscience; wealth without work; knowledge without character; business without morality; science without humanity; worship without sacrifice.
- Mohandas Gandhi

Ideology offers human beings the illusion of dignity and morals while making it easier to part with them.
- Vacal Haval

Act so that you treat humanity . . . always as an end and never as a means only.
- Immanuel Kant, his categorical imperative

Moral certainty is always a sign of cultural inferiority. The more uncivilized the man, the surer he is that he knows precisely what is right and what is wrong.
- H. L. Mencken

It is immoral that some in Congress advocate savage cuts in Medicare, Medicaid, and Social Security while those same people vote to preserve billions in tax breaks for Exxon Mobil which is the most profitable corporation in America.
- Bernie Sanders

In such a world of conflict, a world of victims and executioners, it is the job of thinking people . . . not to be on the side of the executioners.
- Howard Zinn

Neutrality and Silence

He who takes a stand is often wrong, but he who fails to take a stand is always wrong.
- Anonymous

Washing one's hands of the conflict between the powerful and the powerless means to side with the powerful, not to be neutral.
- Paulo Freire

The hottest places in hell are reserved for those who in a period of moral crisis maintain their neutrality.
- John F. Kennedy, (interpreting or misquoting Dante) at the signing of the charter establishing the German Peace Corps

Our lives begin to end the day we become silent about the things that matter.
- Martin Luther King

History will have to record that the greatest tragedy of this period of social transition was not the strident clamor of the bad people, but the appalling silence of the good people.
- Martin Luther King

He who does not move does not notice his chains.
- Rosa Luxembourg

Silence is the voice of complicity.
- Protest sign

You have the right to remain silent, but I don't recommend it.
- Protest sign

In a world already moving in certain directions, where wealth and power are already distributed in certain ways, neutrality means accepting the way things are now.
- Howard Zinn

Occupy Movement

We are living in a time of decentralized populist political movements, fueled by economic anxiety and magnified by social media.
- John Avalon

If you go to one demonstration and then go home, that's something, but the people in power can live with that. What they can't live with is sustained pressure that keeps building.
- Noam Chomsky

I see this movement as a movement of movements . . . I think it's about people trying to create ways of expressing themselves politically because they feel that the electoral channels are closed to them.
- Heather Gautney

The Occupy movement is not finally about occupying. It is . . . about shifting power from the 1 percent to the 99 percent.
- Chris Hedges

The Occupy movement began without pundit predictions, without funding, without organization, with only determined people in tents, countless Davids taking on the smug Goliath.
- Tom Hayden

We exposed the unfair economy and our dysfunctional government. We showed people they could have an impact. We showed people they could have power. We let the genie out of the bottle. No one will put it back in.
- Kevin Zeese, one of the original Occupy organizers

Obama Is Not A Brown-Skinned Anti-War Socialist Who Gives Away Free Health Care. You're Thinking of Jesus.
- Banner at Occupy protest

When fairness is betrayed, when ordinary people just don't matter to those who get to make the rules, it may be time to break them.
- Lisa Dodson

I'm done being the victim. However long I have left is dedicated heart and soul to this movement, no matter what it takes.
- Miran Istina, 18-year-old denied health coverage by countless providers because she suffers from leukemia and needed a bone marrow transplant

The original message of Occupy Wall Street is still true now — that banks got bailed out and we got sold out.
- Stewart Leonard

We are the 99%
- Occupy Wall Street banner

I know where you are coming from. My family was fucked over by foreclosures and predatory loans and the banking industry being twisted ... but I can't be with you guys because of this badge.
- Police officer arresting protesters on the Brooklyn Bridge

A government accountable to the people, freed up from corporate influence.
- Amin Husain and Katie Davison, on the purpose of Occupy Wall Street

You Can't Evict An Idea
- Protest sign in Zuccotti Park

Robin Hood Was Right
- Protest sign at Occupy Wall Street rally

If you don't understand why we are here, but you can name all the Kardashians, it's time to turn off the TV and pay attention
- Protest sign at Occupy Wall Street rally

Why did the government bail out big banks, insurance companies and large corporations instead of helping millions of Americans deprived by the economic crisis of jobs, benefits, and even their homes?
- Richard Wolff

Oppression

As nightfall does not come all at once, neither does
oppression.
- William O. Douglas

Find out just what any people will quietly submit to and
you have the exact measure of the injustice and wrong
which will be imposed on them.
- Frederick Douglass

The increasing domination of corporations over virtually
every dimension of our lives – economic, political, cultural,
even spiritual – poses a fundamental threat to the well-
being of our society.
- Lee Drutman and Charles Cray

Racism and oppression have traditionally been
synonymous with good business practice for America.
- Beverly J. Hawkins

If you want a picture of the future, imagine a boot
stamping on a human face – forever.
- George Orwell

Patriotism

Our country is not the only thing to which we owe our allegiance. It is also owed to justice and to humanity. Patriotism consists not in waving the flag, but in striving that our country shall be righteous as well as strong.
- James Bryce

The love of one's country is a splendid thing. But why should love stop at the border?
- Pablo Casals

The highest patriotism is not a blind acceptance of official policy, but a love of one's country deep enough to call her to a higher standard.
- George S. McGovern

They [corporations] are counting on your patriotism to distract you from their plunder. They're counting on you to stand at attention with your hand over your heart, pledging allegiance to the flag, while they pick your pocket.
- Bill Moyers

Patriotism is often an arbitrary veneration of real estate above principles.
- George Jean Nathan

If you want a symbolic gesture, don't burn the flag; wash it.
- Norman Thomas

From Occupy Wall Street to the Arab Spring, there's something afoot in our society about taking greater ownership of our civic and collective destiny.
- Gary Vikan

There is no flag large enough to cover the shame of killing innocent people.
- Howard Zinn

Peace

Peace is good for all peoples except profiteers.
- Gary Amirault

Peace is the only battle worth waging.
- Albert Camus

If someone thinks that peace and love are just a cliche that must have been left behind in the 60s, that's a problem. Peace and love are eternal.
- John Lennon

Blessed are the peacemakers, for they shall be called the sons of God.
- Matthew 5:9

QUOTES from the UNDERGROUND

Political Parties

I'm tired of blaming Republicans for everything. We have a two-party system. When is the other party going to suit up?
- Andrew Foster Altschul

The Democrats seem to be basically nicer people, but they have demonstrated time and again that they have the management skills of celery.
- Dave Barry

What about the opposition [Democratic] party? Too often they're not in opposition. With some notable exceptions, they've been absent without leave in this battle for America's soul. When one party is shameless, the other can't afford to be spineless.
- Julian Bond

In the United States . . . there are two parties, so-called, but they're really factions of the same party, the Business Party. Both represent some range of business interests.
- Noam Chomsky

The Greens carry forward the traditional values of the Left: freedom, equality, and solidarity. We want to create a truly democratic society without class exploitation or social domination.
- Green Party Platform

Some people say we need a third party. I wish we had a second one.
- Jim Hightower

The only difference between the Republican and Democratic parties is the velocities with which their knees hit the floor when corporations knock on their door.
- Ralph Nader

How many cycles do we have to go through here? How long is the learning curve before we recognize that political parties are the problem? They're the problem! They're the ones who have turned our government over to the corporations.
- Ralph Nader

Our only political party has two right wings, one called Republican, the other Democratic.
- Gore Vidal

Politics

Politics is not the art of the possible. It consists of choosing between the disastrous and the unpalatable.
- John Kenneth Galbraith

The big-money corruption that rampages throughout our political system touches and taints practically every issue we care about . . . This is the defining battle of our times.
- Jim Hightower

Turn on to politics, or politics will turn on you.
- Ralph Nader

In our time political speech and writing are largely the defense of the indefensible.
- George Orwell

In our age there is no such thing as "keeping out of politics." All issues are political issues.
- George Orwell

The political is the personal.
- Gloria Steinem

We need an alternative for people who believe in a fair and just society.
- Roy Williams

Who do you want to be—Mr. Potter or George Bailey?
- Oliver Willis

Poverty

The poverty of our century is unlike that of any other. It is
not, as poverty was before, the result of natural scarcity,
but of a set of priorities imposed upon the rest of the world
by the rich.
- John Berger

Hunger makes a thief of any man.
- Pearl S. Buck

Poverty is the worst form of violence.
- Mahatma Gandhi

This administration today, here and now, declares
unconditional war on poverty in America.
- Lyndon B. Johnson

Poverty is a weapon of mass destruction. Homelessness is
a weapon of mass destruction. Unemployment is a weapon
of mass destruction.
- Dennis Kucinich

If only the war on poverty was a real war. Then we would
actually be putting money into it.
- Protest sign at Occupy Wally Street rally

Among the world's advanced nations, we [Americans] are
number one in child poverty.
- Diane Ravitch

The impoverished serve to remind the rest of us of our
obvious moral superiority, of our wise choices, of our
supreme good judgment in not being born poor.
- Cynthia Tucker

You have 22 percent of our children of all colors, each one
precious, living in poverty. That's an ethical abomination.
- Cornell West

Power

Be neither a hammer nor a nail.
- Anonymous

Power that controls the economy should be in the hands of
elected representatives of the people instead of an
industrial oligarchy.
- William O. Douglas

The concentration of wealth and power in the hands of the
few is the death knell of democracy. No republic in the
history of humanity has survived this.
- Garrison Keillor

The kiss-ass media, the revolving-door congressmen, the
sycophant lobbyists and congressional staffers, the greedy
media consultants – all are dependent on the trappings of
power.
- Don Hazen

There are two kinds of power: Organized money and
organized people.
- Linda Jeffers

The truly powerful feed ideology to the masses like fast
food while they dine on the most rarified delicacy of all:
impunity.
- Naomi Klein

Capitalism has destroyed our belief in any effective power
but that of self-interest backed by force.
- George Bernard Shaw

When the institutions of money rule the world, it is
perhaps inevitable that the interests of money will take
precedence over the interests of people. What we are
experiencing might best be described as a case of money
colonizing life.
- David Korten

Privacy

How can "limited government" conservatives deny privacy rights?
- Jay Bookman

If the right to privacy means anything, it is the right of the individual, married or single, to be free from unwarranted governmental intrusion.
- William J. Brennan

Over the next fifty years, we will see new kinds of threats to privacy that find their roots not in Communism but in capitalism, the free market, advanced technology and the unbridled exchange of electronic information.
- Simson L. Garfinkel

When you talk about the American Surveillance State, what you're really talking about is no longer public government agencies. What you're talking about is a full-scale merger between the federal government and industry.
- Glenn Greenwald

Privacy is a protection from the unreasonable use of state and corporate power.
- Nick Harkaway

In our time, the symbol of state intrusion into the private life is the mandatory urine test.
- Christopher Hitchens

No one likes to see a government folder with his name on it.
- Stephen Kin

The human animal needs a freedom seldom mentioned, freedom from intrusion. He needs a little privacy.
- Phyllis McGinley

Big Brother is watching you.
- George Orwell

Civilization is the progress toward a society of privacy. The savage's whole existence is public, ruled by the laws of his tribe. Civilization is the process of setting man free from men.
- Ayn Rand

We don't need you to type at all. We know where you are. We know where you've been. We can more or less know what you're thinking about.
- Eric Schmidt, Google CEO

Cams are everywhere.
- Bruce Sterling

Privacy is dying in America – not with a fight but a yawn.
- Jonathan Turley

Privatization

Governments have abdicated much of their control over the corporation . . . granting it ever greater authority over society through privatization.
- Joel Bakan

The Social Security trust fund is in pretty good shape today and we should not embark upon risky, dangerous schemes which will, in fact, undermine Social Security, such as privatization.
- Max Baucus

Privatization does not mean you take a public institution and give it to some nice person. It means you take a public institution and give it to an unaccountable tyranny.
- Noam Chomsky

Privatization means corporate control of our schools.
- Robert Freeman

America is ruled by conservatives, and they have a private obsession: they believe that more privatization, not less, is always the answer. And their faith persists even when the evidence clearly points to a private sector gone bad.
- Paul Krugman

America's corporate and political elites now form a regime of their own and they're privatizing democracy. All the benefits - the tax cuts, policies and rewards flow in one direction: up.
- Bill Moyers

Torture has been privatized now, so you have obviously the whole scandal in America about the abuse of prisoners and the fact that, army people might be made to pay a price, but who are the privatized torturers accountable too?
- Arundhati Roy

Protest

I believe in a lively disrespect for most forms of authority.
- Rita Mae Brown

Those who profess to favor freedom, and yet depreciate agitation, are men who want crops without plowing up the ground.
- Frederick Douglass

In the past there was one reason, and one reason only, to ink up: A tattoo confirmed your status as a scary outsider rebel carny outlaw sociopath.... Having a tattoo [now] means that you have a tattoo.
- Simon Doonan

You've got to rattle your cage door. You've got to let them know that you're in there, and that you want out. Make noise. Cause trouble.
- Florynce Kennedy

To sin by silence when we should protest makes cowards out of men.
- Ella Wheeler Wilcox

When we stand up and speak out together, we can create a power no government can suppress.
- Howard Zinn

Purpose

Learn to get in touch with the silence within yourself and know that everything in this life has a purpose.
- Elisabeth Kubler-Ross

When you have discovered what you can offer to others, when you feel that you are on your unique path, when you have an ongoing, honest, reliable connection to your inner wisdom, then you have found your unique spot in the world with all its craziness, sorrow, and joy.
- Susan Piver

Go confidently in the direction of your dreams. Live the life you have imagined.
- Henry David Thoreau

Many go fishing all their lives without knowing that it is not fish they are after.
- Henry David Thoreau

To love. To be loved. To never forget your own insignificance. To never get used to the unspeakable violence and the vulgar disparity of life around you. To seek joy in the saddest places. To pursue beauty to its lair. To never simplify what is complicated or complicate what is simple. To respect strength, never power.
- Arundhati Roy

Racism

The tolerance and understanding necessary to heal must come from each and every one of us, arising out of our everyday conduct, until decency reaches a flood tide.
- Muhammad Ali

Since 1957, black people have experienced double-digit unemployment - in good times and bad times. Look at the population of African Americans in prison. They represent more than half the population of prisoners in the country, 55 percent of those on death row.
- Danny Glover

Prejudice is a raft onto which the shipwrecked mind clambers and paddles to safety.
- Ben Hecht

I hear that melting-pot stuff a lot, and all I can say is that we haven't melted.
 - Jesse Jackson

We didn't land on Plymouth Rock, my brothers and sisters
– Plymouth Rock landed on us.
- Malcolm X

Radicals

What passes for radical left-wing opinion in America today would fit comfortably into the platform of any center-right party in Europe.
- Phil Freeman

Nobody but radicals has ever accomplished anything in a great crisis.
- James A. Garfield

To be a radical is . . . to go to the roots. He who does not see things in their depth should not call himself a radical.
- José Martí

The notion that a radical is one who hates his country is naïve and usually idiotic. He is, more likely, one who likes his country more than the rest of us, and is thus more disturbed than the rest of us when he sees it debauched.
- H.L. Mencken

No man can call himself liberal, or radical, or even a conservative advocate of fair play, if his work depends in any way on the unpaid or underpaid labor of women at home, or in the office.
- Gloria Steinem

I want to stay as close to the edge as I can without going over. Out on the edge you see all kinds of things you can't see from the center.
- Kurt Vonnegut

To be truly radical is to make hope possible rather than despair convincing.
- Raymond Williams

Reason

There is joy in rationality, happiness in clarity of mind.
- Dan Barker

Why should it be socially acceptable to make fun of psychics and not priests? . . . Believing that you've been abducted by aliens or that Elvis is alive, is, on its face, no sillier than believing that Christ rose from the dead.
- Wendy Kaminer

Every reasonable human being should be a moderate socialist.
- Thomas Mann

Thought is great and swift and free, the light of the world, and the chief glory of man.
- Bertrand Russell

I think, therefore I'm single.
- Lizz Winstead

Religion

You believe in a book that has talking animals, wizards, witches, demons, sticks turning into snakes, food falling from the sky, people walking on water, and all sorts of magical, absurd and primitive stories, and you say that we are the ones that need help?
- Dan Barker

On April Fool's people are tricked into believing things that aren't true, which kind of makes it a religious holiday.
- Andy Borowitz

Scriptures: the sacred books of our holy religion, as distinguished from the false and profane writings on which all other faiths are based.
- Ambrose Bierce

Wandering in a vast forest at night, I have only a faint light to guide me. A stranger appears and says to me: "My friend, you should blow out your candle in order to find your way more clearly." The stranger is a theologian.
- Denis Diderot

I do not feel obliged to believe that the same God who has endowed us with sense, reason, and intellect has intended us to forgo their use.
- Galileo Galilei

Advocates of religiosity extol the virtues or moral habits that religion is supposed to instill in us. But we should be equally concerned with the intellectual habits it discourages.
- Wendy Kaminer

If I were asked for a one-sentence sound bite on religion, I would say I was against it.
- Salman Rushdie

Once there was a time when all people believed in God and the church ruled. This time is called the Dark Ages.
- George Bernard Shaw

Reproductive Rights

Free societies allow their citizens to make their own
reproductive decisions; repressive ones restrict them.
- Steven Conn

No one should tell a woman she has to bear an unwanted
child.
- Walter Cronkite

I'm against forced childbirth. I don't think the state should
be forcing women to give birth against their will.
- Joshua Holland

It is an obscenity – an all-male hierarchy, celibate or not,
that presumes to rule on the lives and bodies of millions of
women.
- Robin Morgan

I will choose what enters me, what becomes of my flesh . . .
I am not your cornfield, not your uranium mine, not your
calf for fattening, not your cow for milking. You may not
use me as your factory.
- Marge Piercy

In the last half of the twentieth century, the greatest
advancement in women's health was not ... operating room
or research laboratory, but instead in the Supreme Court
in 1972.
- Anat Maytal

Republican Stars

Romney: I love American democracy. I'm good friends with some of the owners of it.
- Andy Borowitz

Santorum made his very first sweater vest when he tore the arms off his straitjacket.
- Andy Borowitz

On Fox News, they address her as Governor Palin. Which is like calling me "Dairy Queen employee." I was once, but I quit.
- Tina Fey

The reason he [House Speaker John Boehner] smokes so many cigarettes is because his tears keep putting them out.
- Jimmy Kimmel

It's a question that has dogged him for years. Why did Mitt Romney once strap the family dog in its carrier to the roof of the car and then set off on a summer vacation to Canada?
- Neil King

Satan's mentally challenged younger brother.
- Stephen King, on Glenn Beck

He's a stupid man's idea of what a smart person sounds like.
- Paul Krugman, regarding Newt Gingrich

[Santorum's] so conservative, he won't even shop at a store that has parking in the rear.
- Jay Leno

It's interesting what former presidents do when they leave office. Bush is now working as a motivational speaker. And if you want to be motivated, who better to turn to than the guy who invaded the wrong country and started a depression.
- David Letterman

I will show you President Obama's birth certificate when you show me Sarah Palin's high school diploma.
- Bill Maher

I would like to apologize for referring to George W. Bush as a "deserter." What I meant to say is that George W. Bush is a deserter, an election thief, a drunk driver, a WMD liar, and a functional illiterate. And he poops his pants.
- Michael Moore

This weekend 71-year-old former Vice President Dick Cheney received a heart transplant. The heart is working so well that Cheney has already gone to Whoville and returned all their Christmas presents.
- Conan O'Brien

Rick Santorum and Newt Gingrich were shaking hands congratulating themselves on the introduction of an antigay bill in Congress. If it passes, they won't be able to shake hands, because it will then be illegal for a prick to touch an asshole.
- Unknown

Mitt Romney is corporate America's 2012 presidential candidate. He's reaped a personal fortune from downsizing U.S. businesses by laying off American workers and outsourcing jobs to third world and other low wage, low labor-standards, low environmental-standards countries.
- Deborah White

Republicans

Republicans want smaller government for the same reason crooks want fewer cops.
- James Carville

The Republicans are now the "How great is it to be stupid?" party.
- Maureen Dowd

Even when they win, [Republicans] manage to come off sounding like an oppressed minority.
- Eric Holeman

Give the Republicans credit. They know what they stand for. Tax cuts. Guns. Bombs. Oil. Big business. Old boy networks. Privatization. Plundering the earth.
- Derrick Z. Jackson

Republicans: The No.1 reason the rest of the world thinks we're deaf, dumb and dangerous.
- Garrison Keillor

Trying to pick my favorite Republican candidate is exactly like deciding which STD would be just right for me.
- Unknown

Secular Humanism

Secular humanists suspect there is something more
gloriously human about resisting the religious impulse;
about accepting the cold truth, even if that truth is only
that the universe is as indifferent to us as we are to it.
- Tom Flynn

Our government is not founded upon the rights of gods,
but upon the rights of men.
- Robert Ingersoll

No deity will save us; we must save ourselves.
- Paul Kurtz

What I believe but cannot prove is that no part of my
consciousness will survive my death.
- Ian McEwan

That is the whole trouble with being a heretic. One usually
must think out everything for oneself.
- Aubrey Menan

When I was a kid I used to pray every night for a new
bicycle. Then I realized that the Lord doesn't work that way
so I stole one and asked Him to forgive me.
- Emo Philips

Many are the world's wonders, but none more wondrous
than man.
- Sophocles

We are talking about a society in which there will be no
roles other than those chosen or those earned. We are
really talking about humanism.
- Gloria Steinem

I am a Humanist, which means, in part, that I have tried to
behave decently without expectations of rewards or
punishment after I am dead.
- Kurt Vonnegut

Sex

Sex without love is an empty experience, but, as empty experiences go, it's one of the best.
- Woody Allen

When the authorities warn you of the dangers of having sex, there is an important lesson to be learned. Do not have sex with the authorities.
- Matt Groening

You know that look women get when they want sex? Me neither.
- Drew Carey

Sex is one of the most wholesome, beautiful, and natural experiences that money can buy.
- Steve Martin

If sex is such a natural phenomenon, how come there are so many books on how to do it?
- Bette Midler

I have tried sex with both men and women. I found I liked it.
- Dusty Springfield

Women might be able to fake orgasms, but men can fake whole relationships.
- Sharon Stone

To me, "sexual freedom" means freedom from having to have sex.
- Lily Tomlin

My sexual preference is often.
- Unknown

It's only premarital sex if you are going to get married.
- Unknown

Sexism

When a man gives his opinion, he's a man. When a woman gives her opinion, she's a bitch.
- Bette Davis

Woman is not born: she is made. In the making, her humanity is destroyed. She becomes symbol of this, symbol of that: mother of the earth, slut of the universe; but she never becomes herself because it is forbidden for her to do so.
- Andrea Dworkin

Women have been taught that, for us, the earth is flat, and that if we venture out, we will fall off the edge.
- Andrea Dworkin

If you have any doubts that we live in a society controlled by men, try reading down the index of contributors to a volume of quotations, looking for women's names.
- Elaine Gill

There are very few jobs that actually require a penis or vagina. All other jobs should be open to everybody.
- Florynce Kennedy

Adolescence is when girls experience social pressure to put aside their authentic selves and to display only a small portion of their gifts.
- Mary Pipher

Men's participation in the domestic sphere is largely discussed as optional, while women's is assumed to be mandatory.
- Jessica Valenti

Simplicity

Any intelligent fool can make things bigger, more complex, and more violent. It takes a touch of genius - and a lot of courage - to move in the opposite direction. - Albert Einstein

How many things are there which I do not want.
- Socrates

Live simply that others might simply live.
- Elizabeth Ann Seton

Our life is frittered away by detail. Simplify, simplify, simplify!
- Henry David Thoreau

I went to the woods because I wished to live deliberately, to front only the essential facts of life, and see if I could not learn what it had to teach, and not, when I came to die, discover that I had not lived.
- Henry David Thoreau

The wisdom of life consists in the elimination of non-essentials.
- Lin Yutang

Social Media

There is a fine line between social networking and wasting your fucking life.
- Andy Borowitz

Wherever there is injustice in the world, Americans will rise up against it by changing their profile pictures.
- Andy Borowitz

If . . . your tweets, blog posts, or public Facebook updates become a matter of interest to the courts . . . law enforcement can gain access to those posts — even if you've deleted them — without a search warrant. So, as always, be careful what you say online — it can and will be used against you in a court of law.
- Andrew Couts

I believe that social media's greatest gift is in providing every person the forum to be themselves, speak their heart and soul.
- Jeb Dickerson

Nonviolent struggles no longer require a charismatic leader – they can emerge spontaneously as oppressed people rise up and communicate through Facebook and Twitter.
- Hugo Dixon

The technological revolution of the Internet and social media is propelling a global revival of participatory democracy.
- Tom Hayden

If you are not open to social media spaces then you are not attuned to the dynamics on the street and you sacrifice both understanding and power.
- Alec Ross

The whole point of being a Super PAC [is] to be able to spend unlimited money on the kind of media where no one has the right or the ability to respond, and to minimize transparency.
- Clay Shirky, on big money's avoidance of social media

You are what you tweet.
- Alex Tew

Socialism

Every human being should have the material and moral means to develop all his humanity.
- Mikhail Bakunin, the basic principle of socialism

Socialism and social democracy today are about a society with more solidarity, more protection of people, more egalitarianism.
- Daniel Cohn-Bendit

I am for Socialism because I am for humanity. We have been cursed with the reign of gold long enough. Money constitutes no proper basis of civilization.
- Eugene V. Debs

Marriage is socialism between two people.
- Barbara Ehrenreich

Socialism is the abolition of human self-alienation, the return of man as a real human being.
- Erich Fromm

A recent Pew Research Center poll found that for the first time more people under the age of thirty view socialism positively than view capitalism positively—49 to 46 percent.
- Michael Greenberg

In my opinion, nothing has contributed so much to the corruption of the original idea of socialism as the belief that Russia is a socialist country.
- George Orwell

The problem with socialism - the real kind, not the totalitarian travesty - is, as everyone knows, that it would take too many evenings. The problem with contemporary liberalism is that it takes too few. How many Americans meet regularly with neighbors or co-workers to formulate questions or instructions for their elected representatives?
- George Scialabba

The greatest country, the richest country, is not that which has the most capitalists, monopolists, immense grabbings, vast fortunes, with its sad, sad soil of extreme, degrading, damning poverty, but the land in which there are the most homesteads, freeholds - where wealth does not show such contrasts high and low, where all men have enough - a modest living - and no man is made possessor beyond the sane and beautiful necessities.
- Walt Whitman

Solitude

Whosoever is delighted in solitude is either a wild beast or a god.
- Francis Bacon

Solitude is strength; to depend on the presence of the crowd is weakness.
- Paul Brunton

Solitude shows us what should be; society shows us what we are.
- Robert Cecil

The right to be left alone is indeed the beginning of all freedom.
- William O. Douglas

Whoso goes to walk alone, accuses the whole world; he declareth all to be unfit
to be his companions; it is very uncivil, nay, insulting; Society will retaliate.
- Ralph Waldo Emerson

If we can do nothing else we must, even as individuals, nurture the private dialogue and the solitude that make thought possible. It is better to be an outcast, a stranger in one's own country, than an outcast from one's self.
- Chris Hedges

The individual has always had to struggle to keep from being overwhelmed by the tribe. To be your own man is hard business. If you try it, you will be lonely often, and sometimes frightened. But no price is too high to pay for the privilege of owning yourself.
- Rudyard Kipling

I would rather sit on a pumpkin and have it all to myself, than be crowded on a velvet cushion.
- Henry David Thoreau

I hold this to be the highest task for a bond between two people: that each protects the solitude of the other.
- Rainer Maria Rilke

Taxes

I've never seen a tax cut put out a fire. I've never seen a tax cut build a bridge.
- Barney Frank

Taxes are what we pay for a civilized society.
- Oliver Wendell Holmes

For patriots like me, paying taxes gives a feeling of responsibility, of being a part of the fabric of our country, of contributing to the common good.
- Joyce Marcel

Taxes are how we pool our money for public health and safety, infrastructure, research, and services—from the development of vaccines and the Internet to public schools and universities, transportation, courts, police, parks, and safe drinking water.
- Holly Sklar

The Internet . . . was developed with taxpayer money.
 - Nicholas von Hoffman

Tea Party

Never underestimate the power of very stupid people in large groups.
- John Kenneth Galbraith

What exactly is the Tea Party plan for America? So far, it seems to consist of screaming at people and working to eliminate the social programs whose checks many of them cash every month.
- Carol Logie

The tea baggers. The one thing they hate is when you call them racist. The other thing they hate is black people.
- Bill Maher

The problem with the Tea Party movement, besides their almost universal rejection of dentistry, is that they want money for nothing and chicks for free.
- Bill Maher

The patriots of 1776 didn't stage a revolution to keep government small. They revolted to keep America relatively equal.
- Sam Pizzigati

Dogma demands authority, rather than intelligent thought, as the source of opinion; it requires persecution of heretics and hostility to unbelievers; it asks of its disciples that they should inhibit natural kindliness in favor of systematic hatred.
- Bertrand Russell

It's worth keeping in mind that the patriots who threw English tea into Boston Harbor in 1773 were not revolting against higher taxes (the Tea Act, in fact, lowered the price of tea legally imported in America) but against the privileges granted to the British East India Co.
- Luigi Zingales

Truth

Truth does not demand belief. Scientists do not join hands every Sunday, singing, yes, gravity is real! I will have faith!
- Dan Barker

When two opposite points of view are expressed with equal intensity, the truth does not necessarily lie exactly halfway between them. It is possible for one side to be simply wrong.
- Richard Dawkins

In a time of universal deceit - telling the truth is a revolutionary act.
- George Orwell

All great truths begin as blasphemies.
- George Bernard Shaw

The truth comes as a conqueror only because we have lost the art of receiving it as a guest.
- Rabindranath Tagore

Rather than love, than money, than fame, give me truth.
- Henry David Thoreau

It takes two to tell the truth: one to say it and another to hear it.
- Henry David Thoreau

I suppose the most revolutionary act one can engage in is . . . to tell the truth.
- Howard Zinn

Unemployment

Of all the aspects of social misery nothing is so heartbreaking as unemployment.
- Jane Addams

As legal slavery passed, we entered into a permanent period of unemployment and underemployment from which we have yet to emerge.
- Julian Bond

The best social program is a good job.
- Bill Clinton

In my right-wing politics of the time, I held that unemployment was usually the fault of the unemployed.
- Luke Ford

When we're unemployed, we're called lazy; when the whites are unemployed it's called a depression.
- Jesse Jackson

Most Americans who are poor right now are not poor because they're drug users, because they're alcoholics. They are poor because they don't have jobs, because of these greedy corporations . . . [are] sending more jobs abroad.
- Tavis Smiley

An "acceptable" level of unemployment means that the government economist to whom it is acceptable still has a job.
- Unknown

Unions

Join the union, girls, and together say Equal Pay for Equal Work.
- Susan B. Anthony

The success of the union movement, historically, has always been to benefit all working men and women - not just people who belong to the union.
- Warren Beatty

Every advance in this half-century-Social Security, civil rights, Medicare, aid to education, one after another-came with the support and leadership of American Labor.
- Jimmy Carter

If liberals really want to reverse income inequality, they should think seriously about rejoining labor's side.
- Joe Nocera

The labor movement means just this: It is the last noble protest of the American people against the power of incorporated wealth.
- Wendell Phillips

The labor movement has been the haven for the dispossessed, the despised, the neglected, the downtrodden, [and] the poor.
- A. Phillip Randolph:

It is one of the characteristics of a free and democratic nation that it have free and independent labor unions.
- Franklin Delano Roosevelt

If capitalism is fair then unionism must be. If men have a right to capitalize their ideas and the resources of their country, then that implies the right of men to capitalize their labor.
- Frank Lloyd Wright

Violence

Much as we do not permit convicted pedophiles to teach kindergarten or convicted hijackers to board airplanes, common sense dictates that individuals who have been imprisoned for plotting violence against abortion clinics should never again be permitted anywhere near such facilities.
- Jacob M. Appel

Domestic violence is not regarded as a crime in Saudi Arabia. The United States should not have "normal" relations with nations that treat women as second-class citizens.
- Barbara Boxer

Pregnant women are more likely to die from homicide by domestic violence than any other cause of death.
- Lois Capps

Domestic violence does not only happen to adults. Forty percent of girls age 14 to 17 report knowing someone their age who has been hit or beaten by a boyfriend, and approximately one in five female high school students reports being physically and/or sexually abused by a dating partner.
- Dianne Feinstein

We're on Sarah Palin's targeted list, but the thing is, the way that she has it depicted has the crosshairs of a gun sight over our district. When people do that, they have to realize that there are consequences to that action.
- Rep. Gabrielle Giffords, Democrat later shot in the head at point blank range

Violence as a way of achieving justice is both impractical
and immoral. It is impractical because it is a descending
spiral ending in destruction for all. It is immoral because it
seeks to humiliate the opponent rather than win his
understanding; it seeks to annihilate rather than to
convert.
- Martin Luther King

[Martin Luther] King subpoenaed the nation's conscience.
He was killed for it.
- Bill Moyers

The danger of political violence in this country comes
overwhelmingly from one direction — the right, not the left.
The vitriolic, anti-government hate speech that is spewed
on talk radio every day — and, quite regularly, at Tea Party
rallies — is calibrated not to inform but to incite.
- Eugene Robinson

Lefties aren't running around shooting people. When was
the last time a bleeding-heart liberal went out and killed
someone?
- Devona Walker

Voter Suppression

No fair-minded person believes the tall tales of voters pretending they were someone else ...This isn't about stopping vote-stealing and other corruption, for which there are already plenty of laws on the books. It's about rigging the system to keep power.
- Jonathan Alter, on the passage of so-called voter ID laws

Republican officials, most notably at the state level, have created several new barriers to prevent Americans from participating in elections. The voter-suppression tactics have included everything from voter-ID laws to restrictions of voter-registration drives to closing early-voting windows.
- Steve Benen

Photo ID laws like Pennsylvania's are mainly about politics, and everyone knows it. They suppress turnout primarily among minorities, the poor, and the young.
- Kevin Drum, a claim that was actually confirmed by the state's House Republican Leader

More than 758,000 registered voters in Pennsylvania do not have photo identification cards from the state Transportation Department, putting their voting rights at risk in the November election.
- Bob Warner, *Philadelphia Inquirer*, representing 9.2 % of the state's voters

Hasn't America seen enough of the exclusionary, prejudicial, vote-suppressing, racial-profiling, inner city--ignoring, confederate flag--waving, Bob Jones University--loving attitudes of the radical right?
- Patrick Kennedy

It is more likely that an individual will be struck by lightning than that he will impersonate another voter at the polls.
- Justin Levitt

The stench of voter suppression . . . Florida seems to be
heading back to those "Flori-duh" days of purging voters
who have every right to vote and finding ways to limit
young people, immigrants and minorities — who typically
lean Democrat — from voting.
- *Miami Herald* Editorial

Voter ID laws, as the saying goes, are a solution in search
of a problem.
- Andrew Rosenthal

Those positions of real power—the bankers, the CEOs—are
not vulnerable to the vote.
 - Arundhati Roy

QUOTES from the UNDERGROUND

Wal-Mart

Wal-Mart's low prices are only possible because of low standards of living, low wages paid to those in its supply chain, and low levels of concern for it own employees.
- Beth Buczynski

Support Slave Labor. Shop at Wal-Mart
- Bumper sticker

I Proudly Boycott Wal-Mart
- Bumper sticker

Wal-Mart is how the 1% hurts the 99%, and we won't stand for it.
- Maria Elena Durazo, union organizer on the big box store's low-wage jobs

Wal-Mart captures one out of every ten dollars that Americans spend in retail stores.
- Stacy Mitchell

Wal-Mart [is] the most famously offensive, town-destroying, junk-purveying, labor-abusing, sweatshop-supporting, American-job-killing, soul-numbing, seizure-inducing, hope-curdling retailer in the known universe.
- Mark Morford

Wal-Mart is . . . one of the worst abusers of its women employees.
- Thalia Syracoulos

Wal-Mart has a long history of denying its employees the right to organize and right to collectively bargain.
- United Food and Commercial Workers International Union

As the largest private employer in the United States and the world, Wal-Mart is setting the standard for jobs. That standard is so low that hundreds of thousands of its

employees are living in poverty—even many that work full-time.
- United Food and Commercial Workers International Union

[Wal-Mart is] a major contributor to widening the gap between the very rich and everyone else . . . Wal-Mart is pushing more and more workers toward a permanent part-time status. Meanwhile, the six members of the Walton family—heirs to the Wal-Mart fortune and near majority owners of the company—have a combined wealth of $93 billion. That's more than the bottom 30% of Americans combined.
- United Food and Commercial Workers International Union

War

Why should they ask me to put on a uniform and go 10,000 miles from home and drop bombs and bullets on Brown people in Vietnam while so-called Negro people in Louisville are treated like dogs and denied simple human rights?
- Muhammad Ali

The ruling class is the only class that makes war.
- Eugene. V. Debs

We must guard against the acquisition of unwarranted influence, whether sought or unsought, by the military-industrial complex.
- Dwight D. Eisenhower

Do you want to know the cause of war? It is capitalism, greed, the dirty hunger for dollars.
- Henry Ford

The U.S. spends almost as much on military spending as the entire rest of the world combined.
- Glenn Greenwald

The West won the world not by the superiority of its ideas or values or religion but rather by its superiority in applying organized violence. Westerners often forget this fact, non-Westerners never do.
- Samuel Huntington

I always knew the Americans would bring electricity to Baghdad. I just never thought they'd be shooting it up my ass.
- Iraqi translator regarding Abu Ghraib

The first casualty of war is truth.
- Rudyard Kipling

We have been the cowards lobbing cruise missiles from 2,000 miles away. That's cowardly. Staying in the airplane when it hits the building, say what you want about it, it's not cowardly.
- Bill Maher, comment that got him fired from ABC

Military justice is to justice what military music is to music.
- Groucho Marx

War is terrorism with a bigger budget
- Protest sign

Here is a list of the countries that America has been at war with - and bombed - since the second world war: China (1945-46, 1950-53), Korea (1950-53), Guatemala (1954, 1967-69), Indonesia (1958), Cuba (1959-60), the Belgian Congo (1964), Peru (1965), Laos (1964-73), Vietnam (1961-73), Cambodia (1969-70), Grenada (1983), Libya (1986), El Salvador (1980s), Nicaragua (1980s), Panama (1989), Iraq (1991-99), Bosnia (1995), Sudan (1998), Yugoslavia (1999). And now Afghanistan.
- Arundhati Roy

Colorful demonstrations and weekend marches are vital but alone are not powerful enough to stop wars. Wars will be stopped only when soldiers refuse to fight, when workers refuse to load weapons onto ships and aircraft, when people boycott the economic outposts of Empire that are strung across the globe.
- Arundhati Roy

When the rich make war it's the poor that die.
- Jean-Paul Sartre

Man is the only animal that deals in that atrocity of atrocities, War. He is the only one that gathers his brethren about him and goes forth in cold blood and calm pulse to exterminate his kind.
- Mark Twain

How can you have a war on terrorism when war itself is terrorism?
- Howard Zinn

Wealth

Poverty is an anomaly to rich people. It is very difficult to make out why people who want dinner do not ring the bell.
- Walter Bagehot

We can have democracy in this country or we can have great wealth concentrated in the hands of a few, but we can't have both.
- Louis Brandeis

The rich are always going to say that, you know, just give us more money and we'll go out and spend more and then it will all trickle down to the rest of you. But that has not worked the last 10 years, and I hope the American public is catching on.
- Warren Buffett

The top 1% owns 40% of the nation's wealth . . . take home 24% of national income . . . own half of the country's stocks, bonds and mutual Funds . . . have only 5% of the nation's personal debt . . . [and] are taking in more of the nation's income than at any other time since the 1920s.
- Stacy Curtin

The law, in its majestic equality, forbids the rich as well as the poor to sleep under bridges, to beg in the streets, and to steal bread.
- Anatole France

Honesty is incompatible with the amassing of a large fortune.
- Mahatma Gandhi

Rich people more likely to cheat, behave badly, research finds
- Headline about a study published in the *Proceedings of the National Academy of Sciences*

It is easier for a camel to go through the eye of a needle than for a rich man to enter the kingdom of heaven.
- Jesus

When a man tells you that he got rich through hard work, ask him: "Whose?"
- Don Marquis

If we are going to end welfare, the rich should be the first to lose it.
- Mac Morgan

If you want to know what God thinks of money, just look at the people he gave it to.
- Dorothy Parker

We have people in this country who are richer than whole countries.
- Kurt Vonnegut

Wisdom

Though we travel the world over to find the beautiful, we must carry it with us or we find it not.
- Ralph Waldo Emerson

We must live together as brothers or perish together as fools.
- Martin Luther King

If we could read the secret history of our enemies, we should find in each man's life sorrow and suffering enough to disarm all hostility.
- Henry Wadsworth Longfellow

No man was ever wise by chance.
- Seneca

It is difficult to get a man to understand something, when his salary depends upon his not understanding it!
- Upton Sinclair

The perfect is the enemy of the good.
- Voltaire

The best lack conviction, while the worst are full of passionate intensity.
- William Butler Yeats

Women

Women will not simply be mainstreamed into the polluted stream. Women are changing the stream, making it clean and green and safe for all.
- Bella Abzug

The bishops and the Vatican care passionately about putting women in chastity belts. Yet they let unchaste priests run wild for decades, unconcerned about the generations of children who were violated and raped and passed around like communion wine.
- Maureen Dowd

No phallic hero, no matter what he does to himself or to another to prove his courage, ever matches the solitary, existential courage of the woman who gives birth.
- Andrea Dworkin

Women do not change institutions simply by assimilating into them. We need a feminism that teaches a woman to say no - not just to the date rapist or overly insistent boyfriend but, when necessary, to the military or corporate hierarchy within which she finds herself.
- Barbara Ehrenreich

Above all, be the heroine of your life, not the victim.
- Nora Ephron

What would happen if one woman told the truth about her life? The world would split open.
- Muriel Rukeyser

Well-behaved women seldom make history.
- Laurel Thatcher Ulrich

Work

Our workplaces, where many spend most of their waking
hours, are cradles of authoritarianism.
 - John Buell

Work like you don't need the money. Love like you've never
been hurt. Dance like nobody's watching.
- Satchel Paige

Too many employers don't believe they have any moral
obligation to pay their workers a living wage.
- Ted Rall

If you want to build a ship, don't drum up the men to
gather wood, divide the work and give orders. Instead,
teach them to yearn for the vast and endless sea.
- Antoine de Saint-Exupery.

I want to be thoroughly used up when I die, for the harder I
work the more I live.
- George Bernard Shaw

A job should keep you out of poverty, not keep you poor.
- Paul Sherry

Stupid Rightwing Quotes

Birth Control

Viagra actually answers a medical problem . . .
Contraception is a choice that somebody will make, but it
doesn't answer a particular healthcare need.
- Helen Alvare, on behalf of the National Conference of
Catholic Bishops, denying the need to avoid pregnancies,
but upholding the need for an erection

What does it say about the college co-ed Susan Fluke who
goes before a congressional committee and essentially says
that she must be paid to have sex -- what does that make
her? It makes her a slut, right? It makes her a prostitute.
- Rush Limbaugh, attacking a student for supporting
insurance coverage of contraceptives

Violation of conscience
- Mitt Romney, why religiously affiliated health care plans
should not include coverage for contraception

Many of the Christian faith have said . . . contraception is
okay. It's not okay. It's a license to do things in a sexual
realm that is counter to how things are supposed to be.
- Rick Santorum

It's very healthy for a young girl to be deterred from
promiscuity by fear of contracting a painful, incurable
disease, or cervical cancer, or sterility, or the likelihood of
giving birth to a dead, blind, or brain-damage [sic] baby
even ten years later when she may be happily married.
- Phyllis Schlafly

I think contraception is disgusting - people using each
other for pleasure.
- Joseph M. Scheidler, the National Director of the Pro-Life
Action League

This is not about women.
- Rep. Joe Walsh, at a congressional hearing about
contraceptives

BP Gulf Oil Disaster

I'm ashamed of what happened in the White House
yesterday. I think it is a tragedy in the first proportion that
a private corporation can be subjected to what I would
characterize as a shakedown -- in this case a $20 billion
shakedown.
- Rep. Joe Barton, the biggest recipient of oil and gas
industry campaign contributions in the House, apologizing
to BP for needing to clean up after its Gulf oil disaster

What better way to head off more oil drilling, nuclear
plants, than by blowing up a rig?
- Rush Limbaugh, blaming environmentalists

The ocean will take care of this on its own if it was left
alone and left out there. It's natural. It's as natural as the
ocean water is.
- Rush Limbaugh, on the oil catastrophe in the Gulf of
Mexico

Accidents happen.
- Sen. Joe Lieberman

Drill Baby Drill
- Sarah Palin, promoting offshore drilling during the oil
disaster

What I don't like from the president's administration is this
sort of, I'll put my boot heel on the throat of BP. I think
that sounds really un-American in his criticism of
business.
- Sen. Rand Paul

There's no one who wants this over more than I do. I would like my life back.
- British Petroleum CEO Tony Hayward, on his personal discomfort, not to mention that his oil company's disaster killed 11 people

Cruelty

If you've seen one city slum you've seen them all.
- Spiro T. Agnew

My grandmother . . . told me as a small child to quit feeding stray animals. You know why? Because they breed. You're facilitating the problem if you give an animal or a person ample food supply.
- South Carolina Lt. Gov. Andre Bauer, opposing food stamps and subsidized school lunches for the poor

You know, people are poor in America . . . not because they lack money; they're poor because they lack values, morals and ethics. And if government can't teach and instill that, we're wasting our time simply giving poor people money.
- Radio personality Bill Cunningham

I'm not concerned about the very poor.
- Mitt Romney

I like being able to fire people who provide services to me.
- Mitt Romney

There is income inequality in America. There always has been and, hopefully ... there always will be.
- Rick Santorum

I don't care what the unemployment rate is going to be. It doesn't matter to me.
- Rick Santorum

Dumb

Rarely is the question asked: Is our children learning?
- George W. Bush

I believe the kids could mop the floor and clean up the
bathroom and get paid for it, and it would be OK.
- Newt Gingrich, proposing to have children replace the
janitors in schools

Could it be that man-made global warming is the greatest
hoax ever perpetrated on the American people? It sure
sounds like it.
- Sen. James M. Inhofe

All of 'em, any of 'em that have been in front of me over all
these years.
- Sarah Palin, in an interview with Katie Couric, unable to
name a single newspaper or magazine she reads

Refudiate . . . Shakespeare liked to coin new words too.
- Sarah Palin, equating her illiteracy with literary genius

It's three agencies of government, when I get there, that are
gone: Commerce, Education and the – what's the third one
there? Let's see. ... OK. So Commerce, Education and the --
. . . The third agency of government I would -- I would do
away with the Education, the ... Commerce and – let's see
-- I can't. The third one, I can't. Sorry. Oops.
- Rick Perry, debate brain freeze

Republicans understand the importance of bondage
between a mother and child.
- Dan Quayle

I love this state. The trees are the right height.
- Mitt Romney

Mornin' y'all! Good to be with ya. I got started right this
morning with a biscuit and some cheesy grits.
- Mitt Romney, pandering for southern votes

Dumber

I will tell you that I had a mother last night come up to me here in Tampa, Florida, after the debate and tell me that her little daughter took that vaccine, that injection, and she suffered from mental retardation thereafter.
- Michele Bachmann, on the life-saving HPV vaccine which protects against cervical cancer

This president I think has exposed himself over and over again as a guy who has a deep-seated hatred for white people or the white culture.
- Glenn Beck

The Great War of Yankee Aggression
- Georgia Rep. Paul Broun's take on the Civil War

Nothing is more important in the face of war than cutting taxes.
- Republican Majority Leader Tom Delay

I guarantee it's one of their long-term goals, to have one sort of borderless mass continent.
- Senator Rand Paul, on a US conspiracy to merge with Mexico and Canada

The right to privacy . . . doesn't exist, in my opinion, in the United States Constitution.
- Rick Santorum

I have people that have been studying [Obama's birth certificate] and they cannot believe what they're finding ... I would like to have him show his birth certificate, and can I be honest with you, I hope he can. Because if he can't, if he can't, if he wasn't born in this country, which is a real possibility... then he has pulled one of the great cons in the history of politics.
- Donald Trump

Voter ID - which is going to allow Gov. Romney to win the state of Pennsylvania – done.
- Mike Turzai, Pennsylvania House Republican leader, on the real intent of voter ID laws

Environment

Carbon dioxide is portrayed as harmful. But there isn't even one study that can be produced that shows that carbon dioxide is a harmful gas.
- Rep. Michelle Bachmann

God says, "Earth is yours. Take it. Rape it. It's yours."
- Ann Coulter

There's no scientific proof that global warming even exists.
- Jonathan Hoenig, Fox News analyst

I love that smell of the emissions!
- Sarah Palin, at a motorcycle rally

Environmentalists are a socialist group . . . They are not Americans, never have been Americans, never will be Americans.
- Rep. Don Young

We don't have to protect the environment, the second coming is at hand.
- James Watt

Foreign Policy

They [China] have indicated that they're trying to develop nuclear capability and they want to develop more aircraft carriers like we have. So yes, we have to consider them a military threat.
- Herman Cain, not realizing that China has had nuclear weapons for over 50 years

I'm ready for the 'gotcha' questions and they're already starting to come. And when they ask me who is the president of Ubeki-beki-beki-beki-stan-stan. I'm going to say, you know, I don't know. Do you know?
- Herman Cain

Obviously, we've got to stand with our North Korean allies.
- Sarah Palin, on how she would handle the current hostilities between the two Koreas

They are also building schools for the Afghan children so that there is hope and opportunity in our neighboring country of Afghanistan.
- Sarah Palin

They're our next door neighbors and you can actually see Russia from land here in Alaska, from an island in Alaska.
- Sarah Palin, on her Russian foreign policy credentials

I was recently on a tour of Latin America, and the only regret I have was that I didn't study Latin harder in school so I could converse with those people.
- Dan Quayle

Gays and Lesbians

If you're involved in the gay and lesbian lifestyle, it's bondage. It is personal bondage, personal despair and personal enslavement.
- Rep. Michele Bachmann

As a mother, I know that homosexuals cannot biologically reproduce children; therefore, they must recruit our children.
- Anita Bryant

It will lead to alcohol use, adultery, fraternization, and body art.
- Sen. Saxby Chambliss, on the consequences of repealing of "Don't ask, don't tell"

There is a strong undercurrent of pedophilia in the homosexual subculture. Homosexual activists . . . want to encourage a promiscuous society - and the best place to start is with a young and credulous captive audience in the public schools.
- Robert Knight, Family Research Council

If the Supreme Court says that you have the right to consensual sex within your home, then you have the right to bigamy, you have the right to polygamy, you have the right to incest, you have the right to adultery. You have the right to anything ... That's not to pick on homosexuality. It's not, you know, man on child, man on dog, or whatever the case may be.
- Rick Santorum

If gay and lesbian people are given civil rights, then everyone will want them!
- Unknown

Health Care

Under no certain circumstances will I give the government control over my body and my health care decisions.
- Rep. Michele Bachmann, a pro-lifer, criticizing Obamacare, completely tone deaf to her use of pro-choice rhetoric

I believe we have more to fear from the potential of that bill [Obamacare] passing than we do from any terrorist right now in any country.
- Rep. Virginia Foxx

He is an enemy of humanity.
- Rep. Trent Franks, on Obama's decision to fund international family planning organizations

Before we all started having health care, in the olden days, our grandparents, they would bring a chicken to the doctor. They would say, 'I'll paint your house.' I mean,

that's the old days of what people would do to get health care with your doctors.
- Sue Lowden, Republican Senate candidate in Nevada, on how the health care system should work

Exercise freaks . . . are the ones putting stress on the health care system.
- Rush Limbaugh.

The America I know and love is not one in which my parents or my baby with Down Syndrome will have to stand in front of Obama's death panel.
- Sarah Palin, Facebook posting making her most preposterous claim about Obamacare,

We used to hustle over the border for health care we received in Canada. And I think now, isn't that ironic?
- Sarah Palin, admitting her preference for an government system approach she now dismisses as socialized medicine

Just because a couple people on the Supreme Court declare something to be "constitutional" does not make it so.
- Rand Paul, on the court upholding the constitutionality of Obamacare.

Planned Parenthood, we're going to get rid of that.
- Mitt Romney

Guns

Guns cause crime like flies cause garbage.
- Anonymous

I'm actually for gun control — use both hands.
- Rick Perry

I went to the movie this weekend with a gun. And surprise, surprise, I didn't kill anybody!
- Glenn Beck

History

You're the state where the shot was heard around the
world at Lexington and Concord.
- Rep. Michele Bachmann, remarks made in Lexington,
New Hampshire, except the Revolutionary War began, not
in New Hampshire's capital, but in Lexington and Concord,
Massachusetts.

[The Founders] worked tirelessly until slavery was no more
in the United States . . . men like John Quincy Adams, who
would not rest until slavery was extinguished in the
country.
- Rep. Michele Bachmann, except that some Founding
Fathers owned slaves, and John Quincy Adams was not
one of the Founding Fathers

He who warned, uh, the British that they weren't gonna be
takin' away our arms, uh, by ringing those bells, and um,
makin' sure as he's riding his horse through town to send
those warning shots and bells that we were going to be
sure and we were going to be free, and we were going to be
armed.
- Sarah Palin, struggling to explain Paul Revere

Well, let's see. There's — of course in the great history of
America there have been rulings that there's never going to
be absolute consensus by every American, and there are
those issues, again, like Roe v. Wade, where I believe are
best held on a state level and addressed there. So, you
know, going through the history of America, there would be
others but . . .
- Sarah Palin, unable to name a Supreme Court decision
she disagreed with besides Roe vs. Wade

The Holocaust was an obscene period in our nation's
history. I mean in this century's history. But we all lived in
this century. I didn't live in this century.
- Dan Quayle

QUOTES from the UNDERGROUND

Nazis

Individual of great courage.
- Former Republican presidential candidate Pat Buchanan, on Adolf Hitler

They were doing what they thought was right for their country.
- GOP Tea Party favorite Rich Iott, defending Nazi soldiers who served in the 5th SS Wiking Panzer Division, whom he dressed up as while taking part in a Nazi re-enactment group

I admire Hitler because he came from being a little man with almost no formal education, up to the power. I admire him for being such a good public speaker and for what he did with it.
- Arnold Schwarzenegger

Many experts predict that, if current trends continue, whites will be a minority in the United States by 2050; some predict it can happen sooner. If this prediction comes true, it will be catastrophic to our country and wellbeing.
- Steve Smith, Neo-Nazi elected to represent the Republican Party as a committeeman in Luzerne County, PA.

Occupy Wall Street

Capitalists, if you think that you can play footsies with these people, you're wrong. They will come for you and drag you into the streets and kill you.
- Glenn Beck, regarding Occupy activists

I for one am increasingly concerned about the growing mobs occupying Wall Street and the other cities across the country.
- Eric Cantor, House Republican Majority Leader

Deranged rich kids and aging hippies
- Officer James W. Carnell, editor of the Boston Police
Department's union newspaper, on Occupy Wall Street
protesters

Pure, Genuine Parasites
- Rush Limbaugh, regarding Occupy protesters

Lunatics of The Left Wing
- Fox News on-screen graphic regarding Occupy protesters

It's the fringe of the fringe of the fringe. That's who is down
there demonstrating.
- Stuart Varney, Fox News business host

If you put every single left-wing cause into a blender, this
is the sludge you'd get.
- Jesse Watters, Fox News reporter

Racism and Bigotry

We just want Jews to be perfected, as they say.
- Ann Coulter, on the superiority of Christians

Stay out of heavily black neighborhoods . . . Do not attend
events likely to draw a lot of blacks . . . If you are at some
public event at which the number of blacks suddenly
swells, leave as quickly as possible.
- John Derbyshire, writer for the *National Review*

Teabaggers Chant 'Nigger' at John Lewis; Scream 'Faggot'
at Barney Frank; Spit on Emanuel Cleaver; Mock Anthony
'Schlomo Weiner'
- Headline, as congressmen exited the Capitol

If Obama weren't black he'd be a tour guide in Honolulu.
- Rush Limbaugh

Let the unskilled jobs that take absolutely no knowledge whatsoever to do — let stupid and unskilled Mexicans do that work.
- Rush Limbaugh

Niggerhead
- Name of Rick Perry's family campground

There are times when an abortion is necessary. I know that. When you have a black and a white. Or a rape.
- Richard Nixon

I think it's a bad business decision to exclude anybody from your restaurant — but, at the same time, I do believe in private ownership.
- GOP Senator Rand Paul, on why the government shouldn't require private businesses to serve customers of all races

Darkies are wonderful people, and they have their place in our Church.
- Joseph Fielding Smith, former president of The Church of Jesus Christ of Latter-day Saints (Mormons)

Religion

I don't know that atheists should be considered citizens, nor should they be considered patriots. This is one nation under God.
- George H.W. Bush

Mosques are not churches like we would think of churches. They think of mosques more as a foothold into a society, as a foothold into a community, more in the cultural and in the nationalistic sense. Our churches -- we don't feel that way, they're places of worship.
- Colorado state Sen. Kevin Grantham supporting a ban on construction of new mosques

Mormonism is a cult.
- Robert Jeffress, a rightwing Texas pastor who still prefers
Romney to Obama

Phony theology
- Rick Santorum, his take on President Obama's religion

That makes me want to throw up.
- Rick Santorum, regarding JFK's speech on the separation
of church and state

Evolution is a bankrupt speculative philosophy, not a
scientific fact. Only a spiritually bankrupt society could
ever believe it . . . Only atheists could accept this Satanic
theory.
- Jimmy Swaggart

Tea Party

Because I do not wear high heels. She has questioned my
manhood, and I think it's fair to respond. I have cowboy
boots, they have real bullshit on them. And that's Weld
County bullshit, not Washington, D.C., bullshit.
- Tea Party candidate Ken Buck, after being asked why
people should vote for him for the Colorado GOP Senate
nomination

You're telling me that's in the First Amendment?
- Delaware GOP Senate candidate Christine O'Donnell,
questioning whether the Constitution calls for separation
of church and state

American scientific companies are crossbreeding humans
and animals and coming up with mice with fully
functioning human brains.
- Christine O'Donnell

I was dabbling into every other kind of religion before I became a Christian. I was dabbling in witchcraft; I've dabbled in Buddhism. I would have become a Hare Krishna but I didn't want to become a vegetarian.
- Christine O'Donnell, before she was a Tea Party candidate

I absolutely do not believe in the science of man-caused climate change. It's not proven by any stretch of the imagination . . . It's far more likely that it's just sunspot activity or just something in the geologic eons of time. Excess carbon dioxide in the atmosphere 'gets sucked down by trees and helps the trees grow.
- Ron Johnson, Wisconsin Tea Party-backed Senate candidate

Baby Killer!
- Rep. Randy Neugebauer, member of the Tea Party Caucus, shouting at Rep. Bart Stupak as he spoke on the House floor during the health care vote

The greatest threat to America is not necessarily a recession or even another terrorist attack. The greatest threat to America is a liberal media bias.
- Rep. Lamar Smith

The exact phrase 'separation of Church and State' came out of Adolph Hitler's mouth, that's where it comes from. So the next time your liberal friends talk about the separation of Church and State, ask them why they're Nazis.
- Glen Urquhart, Tea Party-backed nominee for the Delaware House

It's time groups like the NAACP went to the trash heap of history where they belong with all the other vile racist groups that emerged in our history.
- Mark Williams, spokesman for the Tea Party Express

You lie!
- Rep. Joe Wilson, member of the Tea Party Caucus, shouting at President Obama during his address before a joint session of Congress

Violence

I'm thinking about killing Michael Moore, and I'm wondering if I could kill him myself, or if I would need to hire somebody to do it.
- Glenn Beck

Our nation was founded on violence. The option is on the table. I don't think that we should ever remove anything from the table as it relates to our liberties and our freedoms.
- Tea Party-backed Texas GOP congressional candidate Stephen Broden, suggesting the violent overthrow of the U.S. government if Republicans don't win at the ballot box

My only regret with Timothy McVeigh is he did not go to the New York Times Building.
- Ann Coulter, on the Oklahoma City bomber who killed 168 people - 19 of them children - and injured hundreds.

I tell people don't kill all the liberals. Leave enough so we can have two on every campus - living fossils - so we will never forget what these people stood for.
- Rush Limbaugh

I just wish Katrina had only hit the United Nations building.
- Bill O'Reilly, on the deadly natural disaster that took over 1,800 lives

When I, or people like me, are running the country, you'd better flee, because we will find you, we will try you, and we'll execute you.
- Randell Terry, founder of Operation Rescue, to doctors who perform abortions

I hope you realize there's a target on your back now. There are many people out there that want you dead. Just remember that as you are politicing for your reelection. It only takes one piece of lead.
- Charles Alan Wilson, to Sen. Patty Murray for her support of health reform legislation

Wall Street

If stock markets experts were so expert, they would be buying stocks, not selling advice.
- Norman R. Augustine

Don't blame Wall Street, don't blame the big banks. If you don't have a job and you are not rich, blame yourself!
- Herman Cain

Wealth passing through the hands of the few can be made a much more potent force for the elevation of our race than if distributed in small sums to the people themselves.
- Andrew Carnegie

The corporation cannot be ethical, its only responsibility is to make a profit.
- Milton Freidman

Corporations are people, my friend... of course they are. Everything corporations earn ultimately goes to the people. Where do you think it goes? Whose pockets? Whose pockets? People's pockets. Human beings, my friend.
- Mitt Romney

The point is you can't be too greedy.
- Donald Trump

War

Go fuck yourself.
- Dick Cheney to Sen. Patrick Leahy about war profiteering by Cheney's Halliburton corporation

My belief is we will, in fact, be greeted as liberators.
- Dick Cheney, on invading Iraq

The only way to reduce the number of nuclear weapons is
to use them.
- Rush Limbaugh

This was a war of Obama's choosing. This is not something
the United States has actively prosecuted or wanted to
engage in.
- Republican National Committee Chairman Michael Steele,
trying to distort history about the war in Afghanistan,
which Bush launched following the 9/11 terrorist attacks

Don't worry, it's a slam-dunk.
- CIA Director George Tenet, on the pre-war case for
weapons of mass destruction in Iraq

Women's Rights

From what I understand from doctors [pregnancy from
rape] is really rare. If it's a legitimate rape, the female body
has ways to try to shut that whole thing down.
- Republican Rep. Todd Akin, rationalizing his opposition
to abortion even in cases of rape and trying to undermine
the authenticity of sexual violence

You just have to close your eyes.
- Pennsylvania Governor Tom Corbett, advice to women on
an intrusive, trans-vaginal ultrasound procedure he wants
to mandate for women seeking an abortion

I listen to feminists and all these radical gals - most of
them are failures . . . These women just need a man in the
house. That's all they need. Most of the feminists need a
man to tell them what time of day it is and to lead them
home.
- Jerry Falwell

I really believe that the pagans, and the abortionists, and the feminists, and the gays and the lesbians who are actively trying to make that an alternative lifestyle, the ACLU, People for the American Way — all of them who have tried to secularize America — I point the finger in their face and say 'you helped this happen.
- Jerry Falwell, on the 9/11 attacks

I love the women's movement - especially when walking behind it.
- Rush Limbaugh, on his selection as one of the judges of the Miss America Pageant

Feminism was established so as to allow unattractive women easier access to the mainstream of society.
- Rush Limbaugh

The feminist agenda is not about equal rights for women. It is about a socialist, anti-family political movement that encourages women to leave their husbands, kill their children, practice witchcraft, destroy capitalism and become lesbians.
- Pat Robertson

I know this is painful for the ladies to hear, but if you get married, you have accepted the headship of a man, your husband. Christ is the head of the household and the husband is the head of the wife, and that's the way it is, period.
- Pat Robertson

Made in the USA
San Bernardino, CA
15 November 2019

59967579R00104